THE FC NANTES EXPERIMENT

SIMON RANCE

From theF**KALLthatpress.

Antony Rowe
Publishing Services

This book has been printed digitally and produced in a standard specification
in order to ensure its continuing availability

Published by Antony Rowe Publishing Services in 2006
2 Whittle Drive
Highfield Industrial Estate
Eastbourne
East Sussex
BN23 6QT
England

ISBN 1-905200-19-6

Printed and bound by Antony Rowe Ltd, Eastbourne

At the sight of the sea, Mrs Elphinstone, in spite of the assurances of her sister-in-law, gave way to panic. She had never been out of England before, she would rather die than trust herself friendless in a foreign country, and so forth. She seemed, poor woman, to imagine that the French and the Martians might prove very similar.

H.G. Wells
The war of the worlds

Introduction

(By the time I get to Penge East, she'll be rising)

A group had gathered. The reason – a birthday. The location – Penge, the jewel in the crown of south east London. Where the sun always/never shines, (delete as appropriate).

The congregation consisted of my girlfriend, Hetty and her family, (Mother, Father, three sisters, accumulated husbands and my good self).

One such husband, Xavier, was celebrating his 31st year on the planet. Xavier hails from the outskirts of the French city of Nantes. You may, or may not, know that this is a beautiful part of the world situated on the Loire. This is probably why I thought that tonight's location for the soiree was a little strange.

As usual with any foreigner I have met with a passing interest in football, I grilled Xavier about the latest happenings in the French leagues. For a country that were, at the time European champions and had only just relinquished their grip on the World Cup, the country was doing a bad job of advertising their domestic league to the rest of Europe.

Like most football fans I knew the French teams, but if anyone were to ask me who the right back for Metz was, or say, Lille's top striker, I would stand more chance of dissecting an orange with a piece of blancmange.

The conversation then turned to the English league and to my team, Arsenal, and then proceeded to make its way round to a subject which seems to accompany every single football-in-the-pub chat that comes my way, the 'rip off element'.

'Everything's so bloody expensive'.

'They're trying to take our game away from us'. TV rights, pay per view, sponsorship this and sponsorship that, bloody nightmare websites to try and get tickets to a game which runs your bloody phone bill up the bloody wall.com.

Last season Xavier had given his wife, Esther; Hetty's sister, (Hetty being my missus. See second paragraph if you have Alzheimer's) a night off from entertaining their five kids. Count them, enough for a team if you ask me; and took them to watch his beloved Nantes. Xavier dot-commed for his tickets and off they went, all of them for the paltry sum of twenty euros. All which worked out in sterling to around sixteen pounds.

At first I thought he was joking, (I'd had four pints by then, and I can generally laugh at a door closing by this point) these were, after all, the team that just two seasons ago were crowned champions of France for the eighth time.

Interested in my raised eyebrow kind of look, he asked me how much it was for a ticket to watch Arsenal. I told him and explained even if you've got the cash it makes very little difference, because of the huge support the club has the tickets are generally gobbled up by season ticket holders, or members who are prepared to sit by a phone for half the day, hitting re-dial and slowly losing their minds in the vain hope that they will be able to spunk their readies on a ticket. I have given up on this, I found I had a much nicer time sitting in the pub for half the day, drinking my gas bill money and watching a match or two, via Sir Rupert Muppet's satellite company.

I explained to Xavier that I had been on the season-ticket waiting list for over a quarter of my life. By the time I get one, Arsenal would have left Highbury for Ashburton Grove; a wholly necessary, but somewhat sad chain of events, and that by this time the average season ticket; unless the chairman has a change of heart, or finds a new religion would be in the approximate region of £1000.

My Gallic chum almost choked on his birthday cake, it was one of the few moments I have seen somebody look truly disgusted, (the other times involving my Dad, a T.V. and Thatcher). He looked at me like I had murdered one of his boys, and then taken a shit in his Mother's knicker drawer.

On a personal level I don't hold my beloved Arsenal any grudges. After all this is the modern game, and any front runner in Europe like the Gooners must do what they need to do when we, the supporters, demand big signings and trophies. Although, I hasten to add I still have a bit of a problem with a player making three times my yearly salary in a week, and the excuse that it's such a short career just doesn't hold up…

By now Xavier was shocked at the price but he was also shocked at me. He couldn't quite get his head around why I had my name on some computer database in a quest to wait almost a decade to pay a very successful organisation a bucket load of my hard-earned cash. After a swig of the brown stuff and a pondering drag of a cigarette – I could see where he was coming from.

Out of curiosity, I sheepishly asked him how much a season-ticket to watch Nantes was.

It was my turn to look flabbergasted, in sterling it worked out to be around £85.00. Now that's not bad for Torquay United but for one of the biggest teams of the top division in France it was ridiculous.

Or was it? Are we paying over the odds for football? We are with cars, houses, cigarettes and booze. Now I'm not claiming to be a professor on the subject of supply and demand but it's quite simple to see that, in many cases, we are having the financial piss taken out of us. But on the other hand, we have always been renowned for laughing at ourselves. We have Cannon and Ball, the French have… Exactly!

I started thinking, not exactly straight, but thinking anyhow.

I'm a sales manager for a cleaning company, so I'm not minted. What I have always wanted to do is write, especially football writing. BINGO! Bolt from the blue on a fast train to genius.

The light-bulb in my brain exploded! I could go and watch Nantes this coming season, the season ticket was so cheap that the cost of flying to France twice a month, for the home games, wouldn't be financially out of the question; especially with so many low budget air lines currently jostling for pole position in their market.

Not only would I get to watch top-flight football, I'd travel abroad twice a month, try and learn a bit of the language and to top it off, write a book about my experiences.

All I needed were my two skills in life; living without eating, and managing to find money from out of nowhere.

Could this be my first beer-mat idea that has some credibility? Maybe…

1

I am a mongrel

The very next day starts with a hangover. Not the most original line you'll ever read but none-the-less it is the truth.

My mobile phone's built-in alarm clock, that has the lovely knack of getting ear-piercingly more evil with every new day that I nurture it, bleats my eyes open. It's as if the bastard hates me; this after all the love I've shown it, charging the little shyster up every night. This is how it chooses to repay me.

After abandoning the thought of sticking the digital bleeter in the deep fat fryer, I wander to my job, thinking of spreadsheets and weekly reports I should have finished, or even started.

Now don't get me wrong, I'm very grateful to my boss for giving me a job, and I realise - I really do - that a lot of people would eagerly get up and go to work to do it but, like most people in my similar half-drunk, yearning for my bed mood, if someone had said such a thing to me that very morning I would have smacked them one right between the dole queue.

I arrive at the office and my teetotal and highly-charged-morning-person- mad-fucker-of-a-boss greets me with a song that goes a little like this … 'I am a sausage, a succulent sausage, a lovely, gorgeous, slippery sausage, a sexy sausage'. Fucking great.

This man is called Peter Tate (Charlton fan), I name him because undoubtedly he will crop up again in my tale but I will moniker him with a 'superhero' name. The world has given us many a super-hero that all have names that end in 'man' or 'woman', and henceforth my boss will be known from now on as Mad Man.

After much practicing of the look-busy-by-shuffling-lots-of-paper-and-sighing method it's not until the afternoon that I remember the previous nights witterings about some place in France called Nantes and me using their football team as my Holy Grail in the quest to become a sportswriter. A broad smile comes across my face but before I get a picture of myself hunched over a type writer, fag in gob and rum on the coaster, this thought is followed by a slap to the forehead by my own hand.

Nice one dickhead, Brockley's resident genius strikes again. How are you ever going to do that? But slowly between cuts, pastes and mouse clicks the idea builds momentum.

Could I do it? Is it worth it? Now a lot of people would think it is nothing, it's not like I'm going on a dramatic search for a cure for cancer. Going to France twice a month to watch the home games of a football team I know nothing about will not be the most outrageous decision that I'll make in my lifetime.

However, I'm expecting a promotion soon and I have been skint for my entire life so far (ask any friend or family member how much I owe them) and have also put off doing a 'proper job' up till now. This is the first time that I have been able to pay my rent just two weeks late and my bills two months late. If I get this promotion, I can sit back a little, afford a holiday beyond my native Norfolk and come back suntanned, and not bankrupt. I can afford to eat normal meals and still go out on the lash, have lunch, maybe even buy my lunch from a, dare I say it, deli. Everyone else in the office does this, it seems the done thing. Mighty White and peanut butter just doesn't cut the mustard anymore.

That evening I speak to a few people. I need opinions, options and good old fashioned proving right. Hetty is not home from drama school yet so I go to Pat, my flat mate, (Arsenal fan), who is probably the most academically intelligent of all my friends. 'Good idea, but...' Oh shit, just give me your blessing!

Pat reminded me we were in the middle of the fourth, fifth or sixth draft (I have lost count and patience) of a screenplay, which we eventually planned to make into a feature film. So, not what I wanted to hear, but, as ever, his opinion was valid.

I need a second opinion. I get on the blower to Matt, my oldest friend (Arsenal). 'Yeah Rance, errrr, yeah, nice one son'. Great stuff Matt. I think his girlfriend was giving him oral relief at that point because Matt is usually the pinnacle of articulate conversation.

On to Nnamdi (Liverpool), the first person I met in London, who just happens to be an eternal pessimist. 'Mmm, why not an Italian or

Spanish club?'. Fair enough but all footie fans know so much about the Italian and Spanish leagues, this would be something new.

Salvador (Barcelona). 'You fucking nutter, you're fucking nuts, you nutter. Good on ya'. Well that was a little more enthusiastic, even if he was convinced I'm an outpatient from the Maudsley.

I should have gone about my makeshift questionnaire with a little more prep work. I should have asked, 'Would you be interested in reading something about a football maniac who, displeased with the current footballing social climate of his native country, jumps ship for one season to follow another team in another country. The team plays in a continental league and the story follows the young traveller from London to France, scraping by just to watch the game he has become addicted to and falls in love with his new club and everyone lives happily ever after.com'. Well would you?

Thinking again, Pat seems to only read porno (genius minds need basic fodder), Matt reads 16th century poetry, Nnamdi reads the council tax bill and Salvador is a graphic designer (words are so last year, man).

Finally Hetty walks in, (these days an Arsenal fan but who knows if she leaves me for someone else, she might swap allegiance, as well as beds. She may one day become a Spurs fan. How well do you know your lover? You think you know someone, then...).

Hetty is a throw-caution-to-the-bin before the wind kind of person, and upon telling her that I might seriously think about going through with this escapade she jumped all over me. 'Do it, it's a fantastic idea. You're a genius. I love you!'

Fuck it, there was no going back.

Anyway, I am a mongrel. What I meant by that bold-look-at-me-I'm-different statement is that my blood lines are mixed.

Like a lot of us, I don't really have one place that I truly belong to. I can't help thinking this is the underlying reason I was destined to support Arsenal. The Gunners have had a few homes, and are preparing to move once again. Once my landlord finds out about my lack of tax payment, I might be too.

I was born in Nelson, New Zealand, which is situated in the north east side of the south island and I'm told it's very beautiful and very boring. So I thank my parents for bringing me to a country that is at least capable of qualifying for most World Cups.

My Father (West Ham) is an East Londoner, born and bred, and like his parents he hails from Leyton.

My Mother (a Sunderland fan for some reason) was born in Berks. Her father (Arsenal) was a Georgian Jew, and her Mother a Russian Jew (don't know what team, maybe Spartak?).

Mum moved to West London and eventually worked for my Dad's first wife, the rest is family legend. Come on keep up.

My parents got fed up with England and took my two sisters, Rachael (Man U) and Catherine (Greenpeace), from Mum's two previous marriages, and tried to settle in New Zealand.

After three years, the third being my welcome from the womb year, my Mum could stand the isolation no longer. She loved London and missed it like Ian Dowie missed open goals.

So we all came back, firstly to East London for a few months. While my parents thought over what to do, my sisters beat each other up and I sucked on a bottle. The conclusion they came to was; Norfolk!

Yes, my Father thought it was sensible. How he ever came up with Norfolk is something I think about quite often. Was he reading a book on the Broads, or some other magnet of East Anglian tourism? Did he think this was the best thing to do, take all his kids and darling wife to live in the witching county?

I suppose if I am from anywhere it is there. I lived in Norfolk from age two to seventeen and look back at my childhood with very fond memories. Although, when growing up things were very different. I couldn't wait to get out of the countrified shit hole and back to the big smoke where I was truly from.

My Mum hated it and left both Norfolk, and my Dad for London; where she still resides. My Dad loved it and still lives there rather happily with his third wife, Caroline (hates football), twenty years his junior.

I met Matt (previously mentioned), a new Mum sort of person and a step-brother (Spurs, Christ!) who was the same age and had the same name as me. Needless to say the Norfolk locals treated us as their own.

Then Dad and Caroline had another child, Danny (at first West Ham, then Arsenal).

So, I was brought up in Norfolk. I'm a Jewish Kiwi by birth, with Cockney and Russian blood, a British citizen and I've lived in London now for ten years. Crystal?

My point is that if anyone has the right to write about Nantes football club, it isn't me.

So you're going to have bear with me on this one.

A month on and I've hardly thought about the experiment at all. To be honest the final run up of the Premier league last season was enough to put an Arsenal fan off football for a while. We threw away the championship to the nouveaux scum (Manure), the traditional scum being the lillywhites, of course.

Although it looked like it was going to happen, nothing prepares you for that final whistle when you realise your time is up, and the geezers who have adorned your wall for the season have to be stripped off because you can't look at them anymore.

It's times like this when you do not need your mother to utter those few, oh so pathetic words.

'Cheer up, it's only a game'.

Why is this said? People who utter that criminal saying should know by now, but they keep on coming like they *really do* have the answer to your problems. If it were only a game, would we feel like we do when the shit hits the fan? If it's only a game, why did we all want to take Diego's hand (the Godly one) and shove it right up his arse? If it was only a game, why do even the most liberal-minded and educated of people become bigots and nationalists once every four years?

It's clearly not just a fucking game, woman!

After that rant, it's back to the matter in hand.

We are now at another gathering of Hetty's family, this time a cousin is getting married. We are late, so late in fact that we miss the entire ceremony and arrive, sweating like Nixon at an impeachment, just in time for the free champagne and grub. Pity.

It's a massive affair with a load of people I don't know, always good.

Esther (Nantes) is there with her eldest, Jacob (Nantes). Xavier couldn't make it but I can talk football with his boy, as he is extremely knowledgeable about the French domestic league.

A lot more informed than me it seems because he tells me a piece of news which takes away my party feeling and injects me with a strange dose of anxiety.

'It starts today, in three hours'.

'What does Jacob?'

Jacob looked up at me a little frightened. 'The season, tonight, starts tonight. Nantes are away to Sochaux.'

First game of the season and I know nothing about it, not the best start to my writing career. Surely early August is a preposterous time to kick off the football season? It seems not, at least to the bloomin' French anyway. At least they are playing away and I haven't missed them yet. But never the less it dawns on me I have a lot of work to do in a short space of time.

But it seems the Gods have blessed me. Next week we are off on a two week holiday to France anyway, another wedding, and then a road trip around the south with our friends Liv and Laurent (both Arsenal). I just need to fly direct to Nantes, instead of Lyon, and meet them in the latter, the day after via train. It will cost a little bit more but I'm already taking two weeks unpaid holiday because I've used it all up, a little more expenditure isn't going to make a difference to those stack of unpaid bills on the table at home. There are so many that I'm expecting Prince Charlie to come a-knocking complaining that the London skyline is ruined.

I find Esther, tell her I'm coming over next weekend for the first home game. She will still be in London visiting family but Xavier will be there. 'Xav will be really pleased to see you Simon', she says. Mmm, if he likes me so bloody much it would have been nice to warn me about the season a little sooner.

Still, it's a wedding, the bringing together of two lovers for the most important day of their lives (until the next one), to dress up in stupid clothes and spend around ten thousand pounds on a do for a load of people who normally can't be bothered to come and see them.

The 2003-2004 season had started without me and there was nothing I could do about that, so I blew my caution and worry from a blunderbuss, started to drink large quantities of wine, stuffed my face with chocolate cake and danced the night away with a dozen beauties (one of which was Hetty, although they all could have been Hetty, my vision was very blurred) and forgot about money but not about football.

I awake with what seems to be becoming a familiar feeling for weekend mornings.

I don't know about you but I have always found it hard to enjoy Sundays. Unless you've got Sky there is no footie on the telly, you generally feel rough from the night before, and work is looming on your mind like a water-starved Rottweiler. I think it must stem from childhood, and that feeling of knowing no matter what you do, school is the very next day, and if you are really unlucky – a paper round.

This Sunday I check the web for details on the Nantes score. They lost 2-1 to Sochaux. Nantes scored first, in the 12th minute (some bloke called Vahirua) and they equalised in the 22nd through Frau and clinched it in the dying moments in 89th when Zahiri fired in a cross. Great. What a start!

Back at work, I've got the promotion, reeeeesulto! More money and more work, one out of two isn't great but it ain't bad either. If I had put some of my new readies away instead of blowing it on, well nothing it seems, then this holiday and trip to Nantes would have caused very few ripples in the ocean that is Problemattica.

Throughout the day I inform Mad Man about the addition to my trip, and try to make some subtle hints about a possible forwarding of another week's wages. He doesn't seem to notice and gives me a rendition of his latest ditty 'I love my mummy, I love my mummy. Why? Because she's got a lovely tummy.'

Wicked!

The phone goes while I'm bashing out a rough introduction for this book later that night, it's my bank or, as I affectionately now know them, Tottenham Hotspurs' bastard child. But, tonight it's all on a sweeter note; they are phoning to see if little ol' me is interested in a

personal loan. This is uncanny. 'It's funny you should call, actually'.
My talent for finding money from nowhere just keeps on truckin'.
Next day the bastard child calls me at work; after a credit check they
have decided that my loan request has been declined (I bet it's that gas
bill). I slam down the phone clearly miffed.
Mad Man notices my sudden change of mood.
'Who was that?'
'Ex girlfriend,' I reply.
Not wanting to inform him that his newly appointed marketing
manager is skint to high heaven.
My special monetary wizard-like powers seem to be fading, I search
the office for kryptonite, Mad Man mozzies on over at the end of the
day.
'Do you want to borrow my credit card for your air ticket to France?' I
knew the moment I met him he was special but I had no idea of his
psychic powers. I hug him, and then jumping with joy, ask him to sing
to me. 'June is busting out all over, all over my chest!'
Genius.
£103 including tax, not bad but where are all these low budget air line
companies jostling for pole position of their markets I wonder, not
flying to Nantes I suppose.
After being all quiet on the finance front, the Money Merlin has
regained his powers. My boss informs me this whole 'experiment' is
crazy and that I'm bonkers.
This from he who sings songs of sausages.
I call Xavier to remind him I'm stopping at his gaff for match night.
Before I head home to pack my bags for two weeks, I do a little prep
work and buy some trainers (I need them), and then get drunk with
Nnamdi (his girlfriend is pregnant and he's decided he is moving to
Amsterdam to live with her).
I awake with the same old feeling, and £150 less in my wallet. I forgot
to mention my third talent in the introduction; I can make money
vanish too. 'Just like that'. Hey presto!
Oh well, it's four in the morning, I feel and look like shit, it's pitch
black outside, I've got a headache and have had two hours sleep.
Let's go to France.

2

I'm Offskies!

With the aid of the Gatwick Express from London Victoria train station, I arrive at the run down airport, which is our second most important in the country. No buzz yet, just last night's Morley's fried chicken repeating on me.

I grab a coffee and a seat in the North Terminal; I've got a while to wait. I might as well use it for some caffeine refuelling to wake up my sunken mind. The woman sitting next to me (no idea what team), grabs her child and pulls him close as I shuffle around, finding the most comfortable posture for my rump, I must look totally atrocious. It is so bloody hot; I peel off the five-pound sweater I bought on the Golbourne Road last night while I was pissed with Nnamdi. I sit, unhappily sweating out my immune system while swallowing large gulps of mocha... I wish I hadn't gone out last night. Hindsight really knows how to knock you in the clangers when you are looking the other way.

I do things like this quite often. I seem to think that as tomorrow is going to be such an exciting experience then tonight (Matthew) I'm going to get so out of my face, I'm not going to be able to talk; and tomorrow it just won't matter with all the headiness that lies in wait. This is, of course, bollocks and I always feel like crap.

As the flight only takes one hour, I pull out my trusty yellow paper folder with green writing (FCNA colours) full of print-outs from the Nantes website to get a little more research done. The site is definitely worth a look, it is very intelligently put together, even if your French is as bad as mine is you should be able to use the site to most of its potential.

There is an icon on the top right hand side of the home page that says English but after tapping on it, it reads 'the English version is not ready yet'.

The 2003-2004 season squad is as follows:

Goalkeepers

1	Mickael Landreau
16	Willy Grondin
30	Perica Radic

Defenders

34	Drouin Stephen
24	Guillon Loic
25	Boucher Marc
4	Mauro Cetto
5	Nicolas Gillet
6	Mario Yepes
12	Pascal Delhommeau
22	Sylvain Armand
26	Jean-Hughes Ateba

Midfielders

35	Emerse Fae
8	Frederic Da Rocha
13	Mathieu Berson
14	Oliver Quint
15	Nicolas Savinaud
17	Jeremy Toulalan
23	Fodil Hadjadj
27	Loic Pailleres
29	Stephane Ziani

Forwards

18	Hassan Ahamada

11	Pierre Aristouy
19	Marama Vahirua
23	Shiva Star N'Zigou
21	Luigi Glombard
28	Gregory Pujol

Manager
Loic Amisse (New manager and previous player, taking over from another previous player, Angel Marcos; who lasted just one season).

When I finally get to the tarmac, I am stunned by the size of the plane that will be taking me to my new football domain, it is tiny, and I could fit it in my living room. Could this be a private plane, laid on by the club who are bowled over by my enthusiasm for their organisation wanting to wish me all the best as I advertise their club in good old blighty?

No, of course not, it's just no one seems to go to Nantes too often. Oh well, this will be a new experience, taking off in a baked-bean can. Still, at least the trolley dolly is fit, although a little angry looking, not much chance of joining the mile high club today then.

Some people never travel without American Express but as I have absolutely no chance of getting a Switch card; never mind a credit card, I settle for the Rough Guide to European Football. Although it doesn't have every team, in every league, it is still worth its weight in gold for background information on a club as well as its town or city. So to swot up above the clouds, I pull out my weathered copy.

Nantes, as most people will know, is a club like Auxerre that relies, ultimately, on its youth policy. The FC Nantes training school is held in high esteem in, both, France and its colonies.

Most of the team listed previously hail from it, and many are local boys from either Nantes itself or the surrounds of Loire Atlantique and Brittany. Some players, such as one of last year's stars Djemba-Djemba (now at Man U, sadly) and Vahirua, the tiny forward, have been scouted in the colonies and brought to the club. Djemba-Djemba from Cameroon and Marama Vahirua from Tahiti.

The crop of talent the school produces each year seldom stays long, and as part of the ever-turning cog of the club they are sold on for a massive profit. FC Nantes' favourite sons are probably Marcel Desailly, Didier Deschamps and Christian Karembeu.

Desailly and Deschamps starred in the middle of the park for Nantes and were snapped up by Bernard Tapies' Marseille revolution in the early Nineties. There they won the European Cup (the only French team ever to do this). After this Desailly went on to Milan and Deschamps to their northern rivals Juventus, the old lady of Italy.

The ground, Stade de la Beaujoire on the outskirts of town, is France's best (according to the guide), built in 1984 in time for the European Championship but it wasn't until the 1998 World Cup that it got the recognition it deserved. It played host to Brazil.

FCNA are the third most successful team in France, which is quite incredible, as they are ultimately a selling club; with eight championships under their belt. The eighth coming in 2000-2001, which again is a massive achievement, as they were established in 1943 and only hit the top flight in 1963. The Argentine, Nestor Fabri, with the Romanian, Viorel Moldovan, scoring goals for fun upfront captained the last championship winning side. Ziani, Quint, Vahirua, Landreau, Da Rocha are just some of the players still remaining.

With a great stadium and a team built on youth as opposed to money the experiment was beginning to feel like the best idea I have had since I left Norfolk.

Landing with a bump at Nantes Atlantique airport, I wander out of the plane and am instantly punched by the heat. The European heat wave is even harsher on the Atlantic coast than it was back home in smoggy, built up London. No breeze at all and nowhere to hide from the heat, it was the same attack on the nasal senses as when you first pour water over the coals in a sauna. By the time I get to passport control I'm drenched.

Xavier is not due to meet me for another hour, so I swing my bag over my shoulder and head for Relay, one of the chain of newsagents you can frequently find in France that sells just about every daily edition of everything (as long as it's in French). I pick up a copy of the daily sports paper L'Equipe and the current edition of France Football.

I grab too large coffees and a litre bottle of water at the airport café and take a pew with some fellow kings of perspiration.

Tonight's game is against Lens, full name Racing Club Lens. Established in 1906, Lens are a big club from a small town in the north east of the country. What I can make out from conversations in the past with French football fans is that Lens is a very British style town, I think they meant northern Britain, as it is a coal-mining town. It has a "very English" football stadium (meaning four different stands and full, I presume) named the 'The Bollaert' after the Bollaert family who owned the mines and the land the stadium was built on. In 1998 along with hosting games for the World Cup the team won its first league championship.

The line ups for tonight are as follows:

FCNA	Lens
Landreau (goalkeeper & Captain)	Itandje (goalkeeper)
Yepes (centre back)	Bak (centre back)
Armand (left back)	Faye (right back)
Guillon (centre back)	Fanni (centre back)
Da Rocha (right wing)	Rool (left back)
Berson (central midfield)	Jabi (central midfield)
Savinaud (right back)	Keita (midfield)
Toulalan (central midfield)	Thomert (left wing)
Ziani (left wing)	Diop (central midfield)
Vahirua (forward)	Moreira (forward)
Pujol (forward)	Bakari (forward)

On my fan trips thus far I have been to some wonderful places, seen some amazing, some good and some dull games. What sticks in my mind about all of those trips, though, are the stadia.

I think I have a little of the train-spotter gene bubbling around in me somewhere but there seems to be something quite overwhelming about sports stadia, and football stadiums have that little bit extra due to the fact that the beautiful game is played in them.

The Olimpico in Rome, where I saw Lazio draw with Milan, was mind-blowing; almost perfectly designed. The Nou Camp of F.C.

Barcelona is another amazing ground, maybe just because it is so bloody massive, and gives the impression, once inside, of being even taller than it is; due to the fact that they built down as opposed to up. From outside, it doesn't even compare. But the Mecca of grounds has to be the Maracanna in Rio de Janeiro. Fuck me, that's just stupid! One huge vat of a bowl, symmetrical and quite fascistic, due to its 1950's concrete design. There I was, lucky enough to watch Flamengo play Fluminense (Fla V. Flu) in the Rio State championship final. A day I will never forget as the ground was sold out and Hetty was with me. She seemed enthusiastic too, it was then that I knew one day I would marry her. Okay, I haven't yet but on my return from Nantes I plan to ask her, post-orgasm and pre post-coital cigarette.

Back to stadia, the smallest I've been to, probably due to the south stand being knocked down by progress and Barry Hearn, then turned into a car park until they could find the money to build an all seater stand, is Brisbane Road. Now known as the Matchroom Stadium, to tie in with ol' Bazzer's business name. I once spent an entire season supporting the O's (again fed up with being on the Arsenal season ticket waiting list). Supposedly the family club but most of us ran off to the sexier clubs in the capital by the time we could say 'Daddy'. Anyhow, it was one of the most depressing seasons of my life so far; its only saving grace was that it gave me respite from my girlfriend at the time. Towards the end of that season I decided that I wasn't going to do this anymore. I wasn't going to travel from one end of the Central line to the other every weekend to watch a team lose or play just miserable football. I'd had enough, I didn't need to do this to myself, there were plenty of easier ways to get away from my girlfriend, like just dump her, which gladly I did, and maybe Orient in their own little way helped me to come to my decision and socially save me. I think she tried to burn down the stadium some time afterwards, as well as cutting up my '71 double winners Arsenal shirt (long sleeve) and sticking it to my local's dartboard.

But here I was in France; here to watch a team I know nothing about, a team that did nothing in the league last season (9th), this could be familiar territory. (Note to self. Padlock away Arsenal shirt, do not dump girlfriend). The cost of travelling to Nantes is, of course, a sight more than one end of the Central line to the other; these next few trips could form a far more melancholy chasm in my soul and pocket. I try to stop thinking such morbid thoughts and keep on slurping the caffeine.

With Xavier, still not around, I wander back out to the blistering heat to take another look at France. I remember the last time I was here, in Paris. I took Hetty away for a surprise birthday present. If you find the spare wonga, I cannot recommend it enough. All I got was copious amounts of sex as a thank you, and the plus side with a surprise trip is that you have to select your companion's clothes for the time abroad, needless to say Hetty walked around the Gallic capital looking like a Latino whore – genius! Plus, there is always P.S.G. to take a look at if they are playing, or just go to the stadium, although it's not really much to look at to be honest; but hey, it's a football stadium.

Wait a minute, I recognise that pale Frenchman, Xavier arrives bang on… Er three quarters of an hour late; still, he's here.

Xavier thinking ahead, and not wanting to embarrass me, sticks his hand out to shake mine, instead of the usual double kiss. We meet and greet. He looks well, he says so of me, which I'm sure is just politeness, as I feel like a bucket of shit.

He stretches a big grin. 'Let's go for a beer'

Uhhhhhhhh. Not really feeling up to it, I reply: 'Great, I could murder one'.

He explains that going to the centre of the city is out of the question until nightfall, before I get suspicious of him being the great, great nephew of the fanged count, I realise it is due to the heat. He apologises but the only place where we won't melt is in one of the malls on the outskirts. We get in his people-carrier (five kids, remember) and head for the selected watering hole.

The mall is a strange, enormous block of white concrete, quite beautiful in a Michael-Mann-movie kind of way.

Inside, surrounded by waterfalls, cheese counters and air-conditioning, we plonk ourselves down for a couple of Kronenbourg 1664s. Well, the only real way to cure a hangover is the hair of the dog, and it goes down a treat.

We catch up, as in-laws do, but we get on better than most. I'd say he's one of my best friends to be honest, so it's always a pleasure to see him and hear him speak his wisdom. Particularly amusing, is his stance on the American government, although slandering *his* government, whether he is a supporter of the leading party or not, is pretty much a no no. He is what I would describe as a sleeping nationalist; fiercely proud of his country but without the knuckle dragging and general bull that can sometimes accompany it.

I have a little dig about the previous French election, which saw the right against the far right; he grinned, a little. As I said a no no. Driving through the countryside back to Xavier's gaff, the scenery around the Loire is beautiful but not twee, it is in fact a very rural area. It's a very agricultural place, kind of like the Norfolk I grew up in but the weather is better and the local accent is a bit sexier. Everything is a surround of yellow and green, like the club's colours. It's easy to see why they chose them and where the nickname, 'Les Canaris' comes from.

We arrive at Xavier's house, a converted barn in the village of Messanger. The barn is divided into two houses; his parents live next door.

To be honest, I can't think of anything worse, apart from genocide I suppose, but Xav tells me it's great, as he always has someone to baby-sit. Smooth.

The room and bed I'll be staying in belongs to Lewis, one of the middle sons, who took a great liking to me, and I to him, on a visit he took to London. I am told he is a very promising footballer and has leapt two years above himself in the district's team. We got on so well, that he decided that he wanted to be a sportswriter. I had to tell him that I wasn't exactly a sportswriter, and that there are far better altars of worship than I. He should stick to playing, because I couldn't be held responsible for the day he was sitting somewhere; fat and miserable, watching athletes prance around him, when not so long ago he could have been down there with them.

After checking out my sleeping quarters, I wander outside and have a peek around the garden; all five acres of it, including football pitch for the kids. Genius!

The garden is Xav's Dad's creation. Xav catches up with me and informs me that his father, Jean-Claude (FCNA), will be accompanying us to the game this evening and he wants us to pop round first for a soupcon.

Hugs and manly pats-on-the-backs-galore, Jean-Claude is a total dude, we try to converse but his English is as bad as my French, so we just laugh a lot. Xav's Mother, Marie-Jan (FCNA) walks up to me and says hello in French customary fashion, then she waits, (she's not expecting tongues is she?). In the Loire region it is not two kisses, but four to a woman from a man.

Christ almighty, parties must be a nightmare, just by entering and saying hello you've already got cooties.

Then comes the test, Xavier's brother, Christof (FCNA) speaks no English at all, so here goes.

'Bonjour Simon' he says expectedly.

'Bonjour Christof' I reply.

'Cava?'

'Cava bien, merci.' You're going to have to do better than that to catch me out old fruit.

Jean-Claude says some thing to distract me; I think he could see this was going to lead to embarrassment. He says something like 'Le match'.

I punch a fist into the air (not connecting with anybody's face, which would have been disastrous at this early stage).

'Allez Nantes' I shout, and everyone cheers, I feel like I have just written my name in joined up writing at school and cannot hide my excitement.

Jean-Claude turns to Xav and says something. Xav translates it as 'Pappi says you are good and you are now welcome to eat at his table tomorrow for lunch.'

I thank Jean-Claude. That should be great, a quick and free bite to eat before I head for Lyon.

On that note the three of us head for the door and it's au revoir from us and au revoir from him.

Jean-Claude takes his own car, as he knows that Xav and I are going out to get shit faced. Fair play old-timer.

On the way to the game Xav fills me in on some current info that I may not have picked up in translation. First of all, they wouldn't have lost the first game if Ateba hadn't been sent off. Secondly, they have got rid of two of the worst strikers on earth and one of the greatest. Moldovan being one of the greatest, who Xav calls Pappi due to his age, and the worst being Wilfred Dalmat, brother of ex-Inter player Stephan (not a bad midfielder is one way Xav explains his striking prowess), and Andre, 'a complete fucking waste of space, good riddance.' Xav's English is very good.

He goes on to tell me that the best players are the goalkeeper Landreau, (Local hero) and defenders Yepes, once of Argentina's giants, River Plate 'the Columbian, great, great, great.' Armand the left back 'so good that he won't be here next season, him and Landreau off to Spain or Italy'. Up front, the tiny Tahitian, Vahirua 'Maramaaaaaaaa' shouts Xav as he takes his hands off the wheel and pretends to row a canoe. This is Vahirua's goal celebration. Finally, Ziani 'a real wizard in midfield, the closest we have to a free role player'.

We pull up and park near a housing estate, the only place to find any space. When I get out of the car I can see the hum of lights from the stadium, as we walk closer in the still stifling heat of the golden hour the ground becomes clearer. Up close the Stade de la Beaujoire really is awe inspiring, not like the vastness the Nou camp offers, but the design alone is far superior. The two ends (goal ends, the Loire and the Erdre, named after the two rivers that pass through Nantes) start low and slowly grow upwards and outwards reaching their peaks in the middle of the two side stands (the Jules Verne and the Oceane). Swarms of people envelop the ground, chewing on frites and gulping Kro. We decide beer is a necessity, but our stomachs should wait as this is my first time in Nantes and I should have something special, like the local speciality of seafood.

Around the main entrance to the ground (Jules Verne end) there are dozens of stalls selling merchandise, food and beer. The place is heaving, as you would expect with the first home game of the year.

The thundering of drums interrupts us; a group stride past thumping away dressed in some very peculiar get up. Xav explains it is Breton national dress, and not to be frightened. Frightened? Have a word with yourself; I'm Simon Rance.

It is time…

I pass my ticket to the steward; I take the first of my many steps this season into the Beaujoire. Once inside the ground, the three of us stand in the goal end of the tribune Loire home to most of the Ultra groups. Although the stand is an all-seating area like the rest of the ground, this is the one area which still feels like the terraces, no one sits. The place is going berserk, especially the over-excited Ultras known as the 'Brigade Loire', with their massive flags that cover half of the stand and their pro Breton banners. I glance down at the emerald playing surface and the players are out on the pitch warming up. Clickety-click, flashy-flash, my fingers are twitching manically, as I try to capture the moment, but I keep jogging the camera. I'm too excited and my shouts of 'Fuck me, fuck me' are confusing my new friends. I must remember where I am.

It's a beautiful feeling. Maybe because I know this isn't a one off, but just the start of something new and good. A huge, warm feeling engulfs me, a feeling that only football can give. It's as if the sport itself is a living being and it's welcomed me to another of its hang outs.

You feel blessed to be taken in by such a respected figure; he makes it feel like it's all just for you.

The atmosphere and the aura of nights like these is what has driven me to so many different places, and it's moments like these that you want to bottle that feeling and take it home with you, sit all your doubters around you in a circle and take out the cork and then, then they would realise in a moment of pure clarity that it isn't mad at all. They would realise it isn't as mad as paying crazy mortgage rates, or eating out in a restaurant and paying twenty times the cost of the food on your plate, just because the flower arrangement is nice.

It's not mad, moments like these are a necessity for the human spirit, it's what keeps us sane when you are working your bollocks off during the day in a job, or looking for a job, then coming home to watch another hundred people being killed in a war you know nothing about, in a country you've never heard of. It is a release, because what you are about to witness is, at the same time, the most important and yet, utterly futile thing in the world. It makes all the difference if your team wins, and at the same time it makes no difference at all, and thank God for such futile things because if we didn't have them the human spirit would be long dead.

The Nantes club anthem, 'The Heart of the Stadium', blares out. A strange and uplifting tune using the Biniou as its core instrument. A Biniou is a bagpipe type thing, which is an historic Brittany instrument. Remember that one, coming to a Guardian crossword near you.

The scarves go up around the ground and sway in time to the tune, Kop stylee.

I love the beginning and end of the season best. In the beginning, there is so much optimism. You start off with such high expectations, this could be our year kind of vibe, and the end is pure drama. At the end you are either clinging on to the bottom of the league for dear life; or hovering in the middle, trying to grasp that final European spot, or if you are very lucky competing for the championship. The way the modern league is designed, it's almost as if it is made so every team can win something. Whether it's the chance to compete in the top flight again the following season or winning the league, or getting into Europe; your team has the chance of doing something victorious, something that will allow you to pour out your emotions and hero-worship your team. I'm sure I wouldn't have been able to be as excited about the league back in the so-called glory days if I had been a Norwich City, Leicester or Coventry fan. But now, whether it's good or bad, with the expansion of the European Cup into the Champions League and the Cup Winners Cup merging with the Uefa Cup it isn't unheard of to end 7th and watch your team take on the giants of the Italian and Spanish leagues the following term.

The first names of the FCNA players are read out over the tannoy, leaving the faithful to chant back with their surnames, this would have been a sure-fire moment to find out who the fan's favourites were, but I couldn't understand a word.

23

Then the Lens players are read out to a mass of boos. Although they have brought a lot of their fans with them, they are being drowned out, as you would expect. The North Easterners are up against it tonight. With the crowd roaring around them, FCNA kick off, with Pujol and Vahirua taking the centre.

A minute or two passes, and I'm pretty happy, as it seems I have chosen a pretty good team to support, loads of passing play, with the forwards moving out wide and exchanging balls with the wingers, Da Rocha and the nippy, little Ziani. Obviously, at this stage of the season, neither side are completely fit. Although, saying that, Nantes were in the Intertoto cup, going out to Perugia in the semi final.

Vahirua has started very well; he takes players on, slows the game down, turns and shoots like an experienced pro. It goes wide, but he is leading the line, which to me seems strange being that he looks about as tall as my Gran and the other forward, Pujol, is enormously lanky compared to him.

To make me feel more at home in my new surroundings the ref makes a diabolical decision, he informs a truly mystified stadium that Yepes has fouled Moreira. It's not close enough for the Lens player to convert anything, but the point is it was a blatant dive. I'm angry with the ref and try to think of 'You fat bastard' in French, and come up with 'Obez putan', much to the amusement of my companions.

It's nice to know that, no matter where you go, there are things that can make you feel the same the world over, cigarettes, sexy women and refs.

Armand is a very exciting wing back, and his runs mean the Lens right back has to mark him as well as Ziani.

But when called upon Armand appears at the back, as if teleported. Along with Yepes he looks the better of the defensive players.

In fact, the only part of the formation which seems slightly lacking is the right full back position. Whether they try wingbacks or three in defence; no one is getting the ball down the right side to Da Rocha from defence, only from midfield.

The crowd are getting restless with five minutes of the first half remaining, so they break into song, another Gallic or maybe even a Breton ditty; if I could understand, I could get some new lyrics for Mad Man.

The obez putan blows up for half time, (not literally, although no one would mind too much), and I head for the bogs – last night's exploits just keep on coming.

During our watering session Xav asks me where I would like to get my season ticket, I don't hesitate, 'With the Ultras in the Loire end'. Xavier expected such things, but warned me 'those drums are a nightmare when you have a hangover'.

The second half kicks off with Nantes buzzing around the Lens area relentlessly. Two minutes in and the face of Xav and his father say it all for two very different generations. Jean-Claude is enjoying the intensity with the calmness of a man who has seen it all before, victories and losses alike. Xavier on the other hand was a ball of nerves, infuriated by this test. This is now personal and I know this because he is muttering in French and he chooses not to translate. I am now simply the bloke in the next seat. I'm not as important as either the team or the game, of course as a staunch football fan myself I accept this. But Xav needn't have been so pensive, a shot is fired, Itandje pushes the shot back out but only six yards out and bang into the oncoming traffic of Vahirua, wallop. Side footer, couldn't miss. 1-0.

I've never seen the French so happy, the place is rocking.

From here on in, Vahirua is involved with everything, linking up with Da Rocha and Ziani, and also with his strike partner, Pujol.

Lens seem to be allowing Nantes even more time on the ball than in the first half, and play the ball back out of defence, knocking it down to just over the half way line. Guess who's there, Vahirua picks up the ball, plays a one-two with Ziani and threads it through for Pujol, just outside the area with only the keeper to beat. The keeper comes out, but the young Pujol steadies himself and puts the ball around Itjande, out of his reach and into the net. 2-0.

A Mexican wave travels around the ground now the victory is in the bag and Nantes then make the usual in-the-bag-type substitutions. The whistle blows and the crowd give the team a standing ovation, before pouring out of the ground. Xav and Jean-Claude slap me on the back, 'Do you feel French?'

'Not French, Breton' I reply.

The love affair has begun.

3

Road Trips, Ricky & Merguez

…Sunday after the game at Xavier's parents next door…
A full on French lunch is probably, along with G.C.S.E. Maths, one of the most difficult sit down situations I have been through. This is an overstatement of course but the gastro violence of the ordeal is a total mind blower.

I booked my train ticket to Lyon, (where I would meet Hetty and our friends Liv and Laurie to go on to a wedding in Dijon, then on to the south for a road trip holiday) over the phone from Xavier's. Because of the distance and the scorching heat, I decided I would take the night train and try to sleep. Going in the open sun would just be daft as fuck. I feel a whole lot healthier today than yesterday that much is certain, however ten minutes after I get up we are ordered around for lunch, which starts with an aperitif. I'm offered Pastis, which I turn down, it's the missus' favourite tipple but I think it is rank to say the least. Then out comes the whisky. Whisky? At this time of day? With my reputation? Are you out of your minds? This I turn down with an ungrateful groan. Jean-Claude and Marie-Jan looked troubled. 'Rum Simon?'

I love rum, not at this time of day, but I can probably just about stomach the navy's drink.

'Merci' I try to say, but it comes out more like 'mmmererrrrkkkkdi'. Uuuuughghhhhhhh, yuck, it goes down, tries to come back up, but finally settles for the guts.

As soon as that is out of the way, I'm given wine. These people are flamin' alcos.

But the spread, cor blimey guvna, is just the bollocks. Firstly salad, all fresh from the garden. The tomatoes, especially, are brilliant. In fact, I've never tasted veg quite like it. It tastes so good and natural that it tastes unnatural if you get my meaning.

The main course is garlic chicken; the poor git also came from the garden.

With mouths full of grub and wine, the tables third, our conversations wander in broken French and broken English, waiting hesitantly for the orally exhausted Xavier (watch it) to translate, it's all a bit Harold Pinter.

The flan arrives, also home made, then the cheese. How come the French have such a liking for something which smells so unbelievably grotesque and makes your breath smell like a dairy that went into receivership three years ago?

I look for the cheddar; no go zone it seems, maybe it just doesn't smell rotten enough to make the captain's table.

Xavier recommends Maroilles. He points to it, and I can already smell it from where I'm sitting but don't want to disappoint my fantastic hosts, I slice a piece off and pick it up.

'Noooooooooooo' screams Jean-Claude, and Marie-Jan just giggles. Jean Claude's reaction was kind of like a baddie getting shot in an Action Force comic, so I take it I've done something I shouldn't have. He gestures me to smell my fingers. Fuck me, that is a wily assassin indeedio.

'The next five to six hours, it won't go away, not even with bleach'. Thank you for that.

Anyhow, it's too late now and I throw the bloody thing into my gullet and wash it down as quickly as possible with more wine. The taste won't go and with Marie-Jane cracking up laughing, gives me quick re-fill. I'm glad the Englishman has proved such divine entertainment for you all.

'Bon?' asks Jean-Claude.

'Oui bon'. Yeah right, Grandpa.

We drink through the day and take a walk around the gardens, again, just chilling out.

Then it is time to go and I leave a thankful and stuffed man, I'm already looking forward to seeing them again, their profuse warmness and hospitality have touched me.

At Gare de Nantes I'm running late and burn up to the ticket desk and pull out the necessary kit to pick up my ticket. Then I jump on the train and wave goodbye to Xavier from the window. Sadly for the next seven hours I have to sit next to someone, but hey I'll get through it. Waving to Xav, quite high on liquor I feel a little emotional, then I'm pulled out of it by something…Something strange, smelly…it's that fucking cheese.

They weren't lying, this stuff gets worse with maturity. I look around the carriage at all these people, wondering where they are all heading. My God, it is hot. Yet people are already falling asleep, or at least pretending to.

If I had got this train during daylight I would have melted into the seat like Mr. Whippy on a crack pipe.

The lights start to go off, so the passengers can relax and get some shut eye, but there is no chance I will sleep in this heat and after several attempts at trying I realise I had better pull out my book. I take a long swig of water and finish the bottle. Shit! That was my last one. I check my pockets for change, none. Great seven hours in this heat with no water, this should be interesting.

I start to read, but the concentration is turning my head into a whirlpool of sweat and it's dribbling onto the pages. This is a fucking joke; it's just too damn hot. This was not the experience I was expecting. I don't know what I was expecting; maybe beds on a sleeper train. No, an oven on tracks. Apart from that early ejaculation moment on the night of losing my virginity, I don't think I have ever felt so uncomfortable.

The guy sitting on the opposite side of the aisle to me has come prepared. He has a blindfold on and some industrial road diggers headphones on. He may feel comfortable, but he looks like one of Altern-8 on vacation.

I start to feel a little dreary, maybe sleep is coming, between shunts of Maroilles stench and having to move my crack to another part of the seat because I've soaked the previous one, but no, Mr. Altern 8 is snoring away. Ha ha, that's why you brought those fucking ridiculous earphones to stop yourself waking yourself up with your excruciating snoring. I wonder if he could hear an industrial digger through those things… While I buried it into his head?

There don't appear to be any drills on board, so I wait for the sun to come up, and sweat. I think about many mundane things and then a great idea comes along. If I never finish this book, this idea will give me the recognition I deserve. 'Simon Rance's Reality Theme Park TM', or 'Rance World'.

Rance World's rides will be as exciting as true life itself.

The first ride when you enter the theme park (family ticket just £99.99) will be called 'The Stow Away'. By getting a train for seven hours in the dark, packed with sweating people and with hot air blasting all over your body by air conditioning systems, you, too, can experience just what it feels like to be a refugee stowed away in darkness passing through the border, minus the fear of course.

Finally, after seven hours, the train pulls into Lyon's Gare Parreche. I slump off the train and look at my fellow off loaders and smile with exultation. The feeling seems widely spread, as there are lots of stretches and gasps for fresh air.

I need a coffee, two gallons of water and a crap the size of Alaska due to my heavy dinner.

I wander to what seems to be the main area of the station and I find a cash machine. I rifle through my bags and a queue starts to form behind me. I cut my losses and pull out, allowing the others to go first as it seems I'm going to have to go through my whole bag to find my wallet. I start to panic, but there's the little blighter. Never thought I'd be so glad to see it. Wait a fuckin' minute, my card isn't in there. I search everything.

Oh my God. Suddenly it dawns on me that when I ran to the ticket office I pulled out my card to see if they could take the cost of the ticket off that as opposed to taking the last of my cash as I was going to need more water.

I walk to information, and blubber in bits of French and English. They call Gare de Nantes for me; the card is there, I left it in Nantes, fucking miles away. The Lyon staff tell me the card will be here in a week, which is sort of good news as I will come back this way from my holiday to get that fucking awful train back to Nantes to watch the

Le Mans game. I ask if they can hold it for an extra week, as I will be in Marseille in a week's time. No problem.

The main problem, though, is that I need to call Hetty to tell her to pick me up, as I have no idea where this wedding is, or how to get there; but I have no money for the phone. The info-desk won't lend me any money. If you are reading this and you work in a station and someone asks for money to use the phone, fucking give it to them because they aren't about to spend it on gear, they need it. I vow, from now on in I will always give change if I have it. And if you work in a toilet where you have to pay to do God's duty and some poor bloke looks like he's about to explode if you don't let him dump and you don't let him in, you're a cunt, plain and simple. 'When I come back in two weeks with money I'm gonna crap on your floor', luckily for the woman and luckier for me the toilet attendant doesn't understand. I'm looking at my photo of Hetty when a light bulb blasts in my brain. A year ago, in Paris we bought a phone card. Unreal, It's still there. I run to the phone and dial the mobile number, it's already beeping ready to run out and I hear my angel's voice. I've woken her up; it is seven thirty after all, but right now I'm not in the mood to sympathise. She tells me it's four hours away. 'But I need a shit the size of Texas', the states may have changed, but the problem just got bigger. Beep beep beep. Fuck Fuck Fuck. Bill Bryson never had this much trouble. I have nothing to lose; I've already lost, so I head out for the sights of Lyon with my cheeks firmly clasped. Eight in the morning and it's already scorchio. No water, no food and no coffee. I look for a fast-food restaurant and find a Mcfuckolds, closed. I'll come back later, they'll let me shit, and they can sell it afterwards. It's a win win situation.

Well, it has to be said that, even in a situation like this, Lyon is a gorgeous city. It's full of Republican testimony, as the statues around the enormous squares gaze down at you. I take a look at my Lonely Planet for a bit of info and learn a little about the city. I head for the area known, simply as Vieux Lyon. With everything closed up and what appears to be an exodus of people it makes the moment even more enchanting and excrement is put to the back of my mind. The narrow streets are all cobbled and it's like something out of a fairy tale, or a Stella advert. The winding streets bring me to the Cathedral St. Jean, which is simply bloody great, Romanesque and gothic, completed in 1480 with an astronomical clock.

After wandering around for a while, my gut feeling returns and I head back to the modern centre in search of a lavvy. I see some golden arches on the other side of the immense square that is Place de la Republique. I head across the eerily empty square and find the restaurant open.

Leaving, I slam the door in total disgust. 'What's wrong with this place' I say to whoever's listening, which turns out to be just me. It turns out that toilets are for customers only and although I pleaded with the young lad behind the counter, he was having none of it.

I take a pew in the huge square and read a little more about Lyon, home of the anti toilet brigade.

I knew it; there's something dodgy about everyplace once you scrape away at the surface. This is the town where Klaus Barbie made his name. Barbie was the Gestapo commander that, during his reign, dished out orders to murder at least 4,000 people. Along with that grand old boast, he also deported 7,500 to death camps. So they probably got it in the neck too. After the war he worked for the 'United States of who are we fighting now, oh him, yeah, he was all right two years back. Strange how things come around in this great democracy of ours', for their counter-intelligence outfit. The Lyon faithful sentenced him to death in both 1952 and 1954, in absentia. It wasn't until 1987 that he was tried for crimes against humanity and was sentenced to life imprisonment. Three years into his stretch he died of Leukaemia; my thoughts aren't with his friends and family.

I head back to Gare Parreche, through Place Carnot; giving in to the forces that be. Place Carnot is another beautiful square; home it seems to a mass of homeless families; all huddling together, asleep. A young boy comes up to me to ask for money, I have none, and I know he doesn't believe me. I feel a total shit.

Another hour, (four and half, altogether) passes before Hetty bounds up to me. Result. Lots of kisses, then I ask for money. 'Water Babes, I need water'.

Laughing, she runs to get me water, and then I take change off her for the bog.

I slam the coins down in front of the woman; she pretends she doesn't remember me. I grin at her, and she begins to look scared. 'You're a bad woman' I say before I run into the shit house.

AAAAAAAAAAAHHHHHHHHHHHHHHH. Goodwill to all men.

Now I'm feeling better I can concentrate on some doting on the lady. She tells me Laurie is waiting outside in the car and we are ready to go to Bersaillin, a village where all the guests of Laura and Simon's wedding are staying in a manor house. This reminds me of my privileged existence, and I take some change out to the boy.

It's good to see Laurie, as always, but particularly now. It took him four hours to get here, but he gives me a hug and takes one look at me and says 'Get some sleep', which I thankfully do.

The wedding reception that night is wonderful, all the stress has gone from earlier. Liv has, somehow, managed to bring her wrong credit card with her, which is a stroke of luck for Hetty and me because she's got about 20K worth of credit on it on it from re-mortgaging her house. The food is great, the weather is perfect and the view is breathtaking (no, really it is). High up in the hills, in an area called Frontenay, the reception is held in a chateaux and its grounds. Lots of people I know come and ask me if I'm feeling better and that they thought I wouldn't make the reception. This makes me wonder if the bird was going to leave me in Lyon until tomorrow. The evening ends with Laura, the bride, dancing around in her dress to some ragga and the rest of us blotto. Genius, life's a good un.

The next day after the formalities of goodbyes and kisses, we are off. Liv, Laurie, Hetty and me on the way to Aubterre Sur drone on the outskirts of Bordeaux. This is the home of one of Laurie's old school mates, Mac.

Mac has managed to get us one night at the luxury villa his boss lives in. His boss, the owner of a swanky restaurant, which Mac manages, is one Sid Owen, better known to the English public as Ricky Butcher, all round lovable market-trader and one-time fuck-piece of Bianca. This is, of course, just a character, but the thing with soap-actors is that they are on your screen representing the same person week-in-week out and in the end, and in the viewers mind, the two become one. I have been warned I am not allowed to say anything about East-Enders, or mention the name of Ricky.

After my second seven-hour journey in two days we arrive, about midnight and manage to grab a beer in the town square where we meet Mac (Sheffield Wednesday) and Ricky, I mean Sid (Arsenal). They both seem like lovely blokes.

I manage to get through the night without mentioning the R word, but can't help having a laughing fit in bed when Hetty tells me to 'wake up early as Pat Butcher is laying on a full English'.

The next day we eat at Ricky's (excuse me) Sid's restaurant where Mac gives us a free lunch, which of course is a right royal result; it's called Alba Terra and the food is pretty good. The town is known as the prettiest in France and is very beautiful, if a little manufactured. I don't mean white picket fences, but anywhere built on a hill with great views and has a huge amount of income bouncing around itself is going to keep pretty nice, there doesn't, for example, look like a lot of need for a council estate around here as everyone seems to be pretty affluent, I'm sure the shopkeepers do okay too, after seeing the prices they charge.

Sid lets us stay another evening, which I thought was bloody blinding as we spent the evening in his pool, the girls both with their baps out. I asked them to take everything off then Sid might let us stay another evening too, but I got murders for that one. After a couple of drinks I wanted to say something about El Sid's Ricky business, but Hetty and Liv toned me down.

'All I want to say is that I love your work, you're the best thing in Coronation Street by a mile'.

'No!' came the fiercest of replies, in stereo.

The following morning and it is more goodbyes as we hit the road again. While Laurie's foot is fully down, he can hold it in no longer; he winds down the window and screams

'Rickkkkkkkkkkkkkyyyyyyyyyyyyyyyyyyy!'

The next port of call is Arfons, to the annual village festival and from now on it's camping all the way (wicked).

We meet another of Laurie's buddies Jacques (Spurs). Apart from the obvious downfall, Jacques is as sound as they come. He wants to make us feel as comfortable as he possibly can and this means smothering. He is the host with the most. In fact he seems to be the Prince of the village, he is immensely popular, loved even by the locals. He tells us that we have arrived in time for the festive formalities, which start around 11.00pm.

The next few hours are a complete frenzied blur that can only be delivered by a drunken French community bang in the middle of nowhere.

A totally professional sound stage has been set up in the tiny provincial square, which consists of about three houses and a solitary café. Jacques tells me half of the cafe building has been closed because they couldn't afford to keep the whole place open due to the lack of customers.

It is the four day festival each year which keeps the small village ticking over financially because the population quadruples from the neighbouring villagers and tourists (who probably have got lost). Beers, wines and spirits are a go-go, while slacking off to bed early is strictly a no-no.

Liv gets a little tired, but marches on to the band's attacks on such cultural whirlwinds as Ray Parker Jr's 'Ghostbusters' and some Black Lace number I am proud not to remember the title of.

I am later informed that Laurie and I will be taking part in a five-aside football competition consisting of ten teams the next morning. I start to feel nervous, Jacques has been organising like a queen bee before our arrival. Our team is to be called 'The Shooting Stars' (due to the fact that we are all supposed to be fucking brilliant. I'm shitting it now, I never said nothing). Now, I personally, would never have named my team that. Firstly, it rings with arrogance and sets you up for a hammering (we could be dressed up like right turkeys and it's not even Christmas), and secondly, it sounds fucking shit. No offence Jacques.

Any old how, that morning, which turns to late afternoon in the spiky heat we whip everybody and, with a hundred percent record, lift the cup, which turns out to be a bottle of local punch. It tastes far better than first imagined, which is not difficult.

The team consisting of Jacques, his friends from the village, Laurie and myself congratulate our selves with bountiful amounts of beer and we also congratulate Jacques' father who yearly organises this and refs the whole lot with love for the grass roots game and the patience of a saint.

The evening is almost exactly the same as the night before, apart from two things. Tonight's band plays The Clash and AC/DC, which is a dramatic improvement on last night, and the wonderful FCNA are playing a match tonight. The game is in Corsica against the capital's club Ajaccio. I manage to get on the web at Jacques' but I can't watch the actual game just the results coming in.

Sitting in front of a computer screen waiting for the Teletype to tell me what is going on is a little strange but I work out the lingo and it was well worth the wait as we won 3-0 and are now up to third place.

Pujol, Armand and Da Rocha get the goals but I am going to have to wait for the end of season video to tell you what they were like.

Our road trip leaves Arfons, and Jacques, for the even hotter Deep South and the hustle and bustle of Marseille. A city I have always wanted to see, not least because I have been schooled in geography by football.

It is well worth the wait. To me it is Barcelona meets Glasgow, laid back, secretly beautiful, largely un-touristy and dangerous (the last two descriptions being of our 'weegee' neighbours in Ecosse). My guide book says 'you'll either love it or you'll hate it', you'll only hate it if you prefer Suffolk to Norfolk, in which case you are a prick and should find the nearest multi-storey car park to jump off now because you have nothing to offer to civilisation in the slightest.

A port city that is a bubbling cauldron of cosmopolitan traits that, similar to London, will only give as much as you ask, so you may end up asking a lot, but my child you will receive plentiful gifts.

This is, of course, the homeland that during the revolution gave the country its national anthem 'Le Marseillaise', via five hundred troops from the city who marched to defend Paris while humming the ditty as a sing a long in 1792. In my humble view the greatest national anthem ever, violent, slightly partisan and extremely nationalistic, (in a good way, of course). Ironically, I can't help thinking that if our national anthem sounded as good as this I might be more of a royalist.

I mean come on, the French national anthem, if you were standing in a crowd of thousands and you heard that blaring out after a few 1664s and a couple of Merguez you'd be willing to die for that too. Here's to the French, fair play garcons.

The speciality grub-wise is, unsurprisingly, seafood. The most famous of all Marseille's dishes is bouillabaisse, a soup/stew with seafood, onions, tomatoes and white wine flavoured with saffron and fennel. It is unsurprisingly rich and, just like the city, you'll either love it or hate it, it's not pie and mash, but hey, what is?

If you are only in Marseille for a short time I recommend you go to the Basilique Notre Dame de la Garde. The view is incredible, you can see the whole of the city in a panoramic scape, and if you look hard enough, Marseille Football Club's Stade de la Velodrome. It is the highest point in the city at 162 metres high.

Again we hit the road, heading for St. Tropez. Marseille was Laurie's and my preferred destination, but we realised that at some point we would have to keep the birds happy, so a bit of glam was called for. I say glam, but we were still camping.

We arrive in St. Tropez sweating and looking more like beggars than tourists, which is not good somewhere like here as we could be socially castrated and never get a table at any of the swanky restaurants in town. The ladies seemed to like the window-shopping of it all as Laurie and I strode around behind them in our Arsenal shirts. It's nice, but hugely overrated, and I started to worry about some of the quality of Europe's plastic surgeons also, as faces seemed to melt onto the café patios.

The coastline around here though is not to be sniffed at; it is the Med at its most elegant, warm and inviting. You can swim for hour upon hour and once you get out and see the baking flesh and arguing families on the beach all you want to do is get back in it.

And then our time was up. We stopped off in Aix en Provence on the way back to Lyon, which is another unreal place. It's all ancient architecture and small streets, the neighbouring city to Marseille and about as different as you could imagine. All of these places need time to explore them thoroughly and Aix and Marseille are two places I will certainly be returning to.

Arriving back in Lyon, willing my card to be at the station, I think about just how vast this country is. We have travelled thousands of Kms and not even seen a quarter of it, but what it has done is got me right in the mood for the season ahead, I am looking forward to spending half of my weekends of the year here.

Lyon gives me the happy ending I have been hoping for as I pick up my card. I bid farewell to Hetty, Liv and Laurie as they are flying home from Lyon and I'm going back to Nantes to watch them play newly promoted Le Mans. Luckily there is a TGV, which is four and a half-hours of journey time compared to the previous seven. Hopefully Liv's upset tummy will be sorted when she gets back to meat and two veg in London, because she has done my nut in.

Looking out of the window as the Lyon cityscape rumbles by, it hits me that now that I have my card I have the entire holiday spending money (which I of course didn't spend) to blow in Nantes. Maybe I should save it and give it straight to Liv and Laurie as I promised. Fuck that, I'm gonna have a mass blow out. What a socialist.

In Nantes, it looms on me that I have to get a ticket for the game as my season ticket would have arrived at Xavier's and he is in England visiting, Esther. The club shop, Planete F.C.N.A. is located on Rue de Halles in the Bouffay area of the city and is fantastic. All the club merchandise you can hope for, and the very helpful Tina to sort you out, she also speaks very good English. My ticket is not cheap, but as there are hardly any left I have no choice 30 euros it is. I'm told it is very high up, the back row in fact, of the Jules Verne stand. 20,000 leagues above sea level, ho ho.

Hunger pangs ahoy, next stop luncheon. Also in Bouffay, located on Rue des Echevins is a very small restaurant, in a lovely spot called Chez l'huitre. I go straight to the bathroom and scrub up. In thanks for letting me use the loo I decide this is the place. I need a steak, I am laughed at. Another bloody seafood restaurant… The salade de Nordiq is strongly recommended by the very friendly waitress and chef so I oblige. Fresh salmon in white wine salad, absolutely delicious. A glass of the local plonk, Muscadet, to wash it down. This dry white is a little thorny to say the least, but is perfect for seafood. You will see a lot of both in Nantes, as they are the local speciality, the fish being fresh from the Atlantic.

After paying the cheap-as-chips bill, I head for a bird's clothes shop so I can get Hetty something. Galleries Lafayette is a chain of up market department stores dotted around France. We had stopped in one in Marseille and Hetty saw a top she really liked.

I find the same top in the Nantes store and buy it. This is not because I am the best boyfriend in the world and always thinking of my woman, it is simply because I want to be able to give her something and soften the blow that I have spent six hundred quid in a day and a half.

With the bird's attire suitably wrapped, I head back to Planete F.C.N.A. and buy the new club shirt. It's the away shirt, which is white with yellow trim. Tina asks if I would like a name or number on the back. I have to admit I'm not usually one for this, but as one of my points is to advertise this club and preach to the perverted, I choose Vahirua's name and number; 19.

The final plan is to find a hotel. The only room left is a twin with two double beds on the top floor with a bathroom. It is massive, and I start to feel a little lonely after sharing space about five meters square with three other people in a car for the last two weeks. So there is only one cure for this loneliness: I head off to the stadium; at least there I will be surrounded by thousands of people all with one common goal.

I take the tram from Bouffay to Beaujoire, which is around ten stops. I remember Xavier saying that if you have a season ticket the tram is free, but as it was so crowded I decide not to bother with the ticket as it is beer money, and this should only be eaten into in the most dire of circumstances, such as paying off cops in Mexico while smuggling cocaine.

That bird, Tina, in the shop wasn't lying, I'm so high up I'm feeling the nausea coming on. I'm as high as you can possibly get in the ground, as the Jules Verne stand is the tallest. I munch on my newfound favourite junk food, Merguez, and sit back and wait for the action to begin. The team comes out to the club anthem.

Landreau in goal, Armand and Savinaud at full back, Guillon and the mightily impressive Yepes at centre back, Berson and Toulalan in central midfield and Ziani and Da Rocha on the wings, but more than likely Ziani will have a free role, with N'zigou and Vahirua up front. I haven't seen N'Zigou in action as yet, so I keep an eye out.

Le Mans are newly promoted and get a standing ovation from both sets of supporters as the tannoy welcomes them to the Beaujoire. As Le Mans is only about an hour away by train they have brought a healthy amount of support and the flares start to be lit.

Le Mans are here for one reason only; a draw. Their play is hopefully the most negative I will see this season, they sit behind the ball, all in their half for the entire first half, as every single Nantes attack is broken down. But fair play to the Canaries as they just keep on coming like a rabid granny waiting for a birthday kiss from her grandson, and she won't let up till she gets one. Sadly she gets nothing in the first half, except blockage.

The Le Mans keeper, Bedenik, is playing well though it has to be said. As my fellow fans leave the ground for frites and non-alcoholic lager I keep to my seat, I'm so far away from anything that once I'd reach a toilet or bar the second half would have kicked off.

An unchanged Nantais emerge from the dressing room looking fit and up for the fight. But the game goes exactly the same way as before, forward surge from the wings, from the full backs, from central midfield, all broken down. Until… The pretty uninspired N'Zigou (in this game anyway) collects the ball just inside the eighteen yard box, flash-bang, ka-put, woooo there Bessie, goal!

Fuckin' A. Five minutes to go and the negativity boys get what they deserve. In a way, I feel sorry for them, but you just can't do that in the top division of any league unless you bung the opposing staff some wonga first. If Le Mans don't change their game plans for away matches soon, they are going back to where they came from within a year.

Well, they won, it wasn't pretty; but it's three more points in the bag and at this point of the season that is all that matters.

On my way back to the hotel, I wrestle for space on the tram and look at today's edition of L'equipe. With the previews of all of today's games they have the shirt and sponsor of each club in the league (apart from P.S.G. and Monaco as they are playing tomorrow) and the amount in euros that they receive per annum from that sponsor. This is a good way to see just how big or small a club is in today's market. Miles ahead of everyone else are Marseille, they receive 6,000,000 euros, Lyon receive 3,333,000, Auxerre – 3,000,000, Nantes – 2,000,000, Lens 1,700,000, arch rivals Bordeaux (the Atlantic derby) – 1,000,000 and Rennes (Breton derby) – 1,500, 000.

Le Mans who we just beat receive just 400,000, while the Corsicans of Ajjaccio receive the paltry sum of 120,000.

Once I get back to the hotel and freshen up I decide to hit the town (alone, wicked). I head, as most English-speaking tourists probably do, to the John McByrne pub in Bouffay. It is a fantastic little bar. The staff are Irish, English and French. The beer is Guinness, Kilkenny and Stella. Don't be fooled by the McEwan's export pump. It's not like it is back home, it's nine fucking percent and after one of these, your inhibitions about talking to total strangers will go completely out of the window.

I make good friends of John McByrne himself, who seems like an all round dude really and his work hand Mick (Irish? I think so). I talk to them both through the evening, then again, I'd talk to me to if I was paying five euro fifty for a pint, I'd make sure I didn't leave either. We talk about football and the experiment. John especially thinks it's a great idea, Mick just thinks I'm nuts. 'You shower of cunts' he says. I like him already.

I wake the next morning, via a phone call from the front desk. 'Yeah Bonjour your fucking self'.

'Where the fuck am I?'

It takes me a while to realise where I am. My head hurts real bad. McEwan's, Christ almighty. Note for journal; don't drink Scottish beer abroad. There is a strange smell in the room that I don't remember from last night. Then I see the culprit; a half-eaten kebab sits on the windowsill, between a full ashtray and a bottle of Perrier. I don't remember that at all. I must have come home and stared at the stars before I hit the sack.

I check out, mumbling some thanks and go to the bus stop in Bouffay where there is a shuttle bus to the Airport every hour. Ah, but not today it seems, great. I get a cab all the way to the airport. Another twenty-five euros down the pan. Pangs of guilt, as I look at all the stuff I have bought. These pangs last until I fall asleep in the back of the cab.

The friendly cabbie wakes me up at the airport, I bet the shyster kept the meter running for a couple of extra minutes before he chose to wake me.

Anyhow, I'm heading home.

4

The Derby & a Little Bit of History

As soon as I'm back at work in London, I immediately feel ill, whether this is something to do with missing France, I don't know. I doubt it could come this early into the experiment but you never know. After a week of being run down with flu, topped off by my bedroom ceiling falling in due to the water tank leaking, I head for the doctor with what, to me, looks like some kind of measles outbreak on my face.

The doctor tells me I have Impetigo, a highly contagious skin condition but not life threatening. I thank him for the antibiotics and tell the missus. Within two days she has it too, so do two people at work, one of which is Mad Man who is leaving the next day for a romantic weekend in Paris with his wife, she has vowed not to touch him until the rash has gone. Needless to say he hates me.

Some good news though is heard from my travelling counterparts Liv and Laurie. The reason Liv was feeling so rough throughout the holiday and moaning all the bloody time is due to the fact that she is pregnant. They are both delighted, which is beautiful and rare for two young lovers in their early twenties (although Laurie is going on forty in the sensible league) and cause for mass hysteria and celebration in the neighbourhood.

Finally the rash goes but inevitably it returns, due to every person I meet catching it from me, I suddenly become very unpopular and my name is changed, via mate pole, to Simon Rash.

The biggest worry for me though, as selfish as it sounds, is to get well for the Bordeaux and Marseille games that are to be played on the bounce over the next fortnight, unfortunately it doesn't go and I miss both matches. I'm totally gutted, more so about the Bordeaux game or The Atlantic derby as it is known in France. Along with the Breton derby, it is the biggest league game of the season for F.C.N.A. fans.

The two sets of supporters from the north and south of the Atlantic coast have a mutual disrespect for each other. I hope along the course of the book to find out more about the rivalry but a friend tells me it is due to the fact that on the west coast there are barely any 'big' teams, and this is the fact they dislike each other so much. I've got a feeling there is a little more to it than that. Maybe something to do with Brittany.

They draw 0-0 with Bordeaux, then travel to Nice and somehow lose 1-0, then back home to face Marseille, beating the biggest supported club in France 1-0 (Vahirua scoring). Then they travel away to Strasbourg and beat them 1-0.

The following game is the derby of Brittany, *the* derby and it will take more than a rash and flu to stop me making the trip to France. I purchase my flight ticket from a travel agent in west London, I'd tell you the name but I think they'd get done to be honest.

The lady who runs the place soon realised if she was nice she was going to get a lot of business out of me over the next few months with all these trips to France. So she kindly forged me an international student card to reduce the costs, what a beauty. Over the next couple of days I try to find as much info as possible to give you (and me) some background on the history of Nantes. To be honest there isn't much in print (in English anyway) but a couple of books were helpful, if a little basic. I decide a mixture of these and Xavier's father Jean-Claude would be the best and most interesting bet.

As far as I know, the following is true, but if you have an exam coming up on the history of western France, don't quote me.

In the beginning…

To start at the beginning seems impossible, as Nantes' birth has been lost in the midst of time and some archaeologists have found the trace of human existence in the city, or town, dating back 2,000 years before some bloke called Christ. After, around 800 to 600 BC, it is said that the area that the city now occupies was some sort of trading post, which it still remains to this day. The Romans (seemed inevitable really) capitalized on the commerciality of the river, (Loire), which would provide links to the Atlantic. But although the Loire was a trading stream, it meant it was also a route ripe for invasion. Enter the Barbarians in 260 BC. And when a barbarian comes, by Christ do you know about it.

Preached by the missionaries of Tours, Christianity arrived around 300 years later and one of the most famous stories of the city came along with it. The story of 'the children of Nantes' -Donatien and Rogatien, two patricians put to death for refusing to denounce their faith. This is seen as the birth of local Christianity.

The Breton State

The 'march of Brittany' was ordered by the Emperor and was put into practice by Roland of Roncevaux. This charted the territory from Rennes to Angers and Vannes to Le Mans. Nantes became its capital. In 843 the Vikings sailed up the Loire to Nantes via 77 long ships and basically totally fucked the place over. They destroyed large parts of the city, slit the throat of the bishop while he was giving mass, slaughtered the congregation and pretty much pillaged the city and then left, taking with them prisoners for slaves.

The threat to the march of Brittany was serious indeed, and it wasn't only because of the Barbarians; the Count of Vannes; Nominoe, who was loyal to the Frankish King Luis the Pious, went against his predecessor, Charles the bald. In 850 he took Nantes, which became Breton; it would stay so until 1941. So we can see why a few of the Nantais believe themselves to be Breton.

Then (you just can't keep 'em down can ya?) the Vikings came back once again, (ten years later) and pillaged all over again. But this time they stayed longer, as they had a fight on their hands. The Bretons, Vikings and Franks fought and negotiated over a number of years. It wasn't until 937 that the Breton Chief Alain Barbe-Torte took back the city, now ruined, and made it his capital.

But this didn't solve all the problems as the Counts of Nantes and Rennes now argued over the authority of the Duchy. Conan le Tort conquered Nantes in 990. So a rivalry was born, and ended in a marriage which made Hoel de Corrnouaille Count of Nantes and Duke of Brittany; his son (Alain IV Fergent), would be the last Breton-speaking Duke and after his death, French and Latin would be the order of the day.

Then the Duchy dropped into the hands of the Plantagenets, then the Capetians; one of whom, Pierre de Dreux, became Duke.

Nantes kept developing throughout the Middle Ages and became a true meeting point in international economic circuits.

This whole period of growth, economically and physically, coincided with the realisation of a totally independent Breton State.

The Cathedral, which still stands today, was begun under the reign of Duke Jean V but it wouldn't be finished for another four and a half centuries. Jean V's successor, Francois II, kept building Nantes to the boundaries of which we see today and in 1460 he was given permission to build a university by Pope Pious II.

It was now a capital in every sense, with 14,000 inhabitants.

Anne of Brittany

Arguably the most famous of all Nantais, Anne of Brittany was the heiress of Francois II and had to, after battles with the French army, accept the hand of marriage of Charles VIII, the King of France, in 1491 and once he copped it she married his cousin, Louis XII.

The Duchess of Brittany and twice the Queen of France, Anne of Brittany, was born in and grew up in Nantes. She made Nantes one of the capitals of the Royal court, and after she died her heart was brought to Nantes in a gold shrine, which is preserved at the Dobree museum.

After the Breton unification with France, Rennes became the political centre of Brittany. Although no longer the super-power in Brittany, Nantes increased its economic influence.

The Edict of Nantes

Henri IV gave his signature in 1598, which authorised the practice of Calvinism. This was really only signed in Nantes because the city was the last to withstand the army of Henri IV.

After this one of the most notable pieces of the city's history was the execution of the Marquis de Pontallec, who plotted against the regency of the country in the name of Breton liberation.

The Slave Trade

In the 1700s Nantes saw its population double from 40,000 to 80,000 and for a while became the leading port in France, thanks to the commerciality of Nantes but mainly to the slave trade. All you have to do is look at the Graslin theatre and the mansions around the city and you can see the considerable wealth that it received over this time. In the mid 17th century, ships from Nantes had become used to the voyage across the Atlantic to the Caribbean where the colonists were producing tobacco and sugar. But in the early 18th century lots of the ship owners discovered that one way trading wasn't as profitable as triangular trading. So the ships would leave Nantes loaded up with guns, spirits, cloth and glass trinkets and exchanged them in Guinea and Angola for slaves, who would then be sold in the Caribbean for sugar and coffee. The circuit trip would last for fourteen to eighteen months and made a fortune for Nantes, along with Liverpool, Amsterdam and Lisbon. Nantes became one of the main centres of the slave trade to the point when every other slave ship in France would come from Nantes. Four hundred and fifty thousand slaves were shipped from Africa to America from Loire departed vessels. There is a saying that the buildings of Nantes smell of black sweat. Although the slaves never set foot on Nantais soil, their work and suffering helped build the majority of the city as you see it today. Mayor of Nantes from 1720 to 1729, Gerard Mellier gave this verdict/excuse - "Negritia is a large region of Africa divided into several kingdoms whose populations are so dense that it would be difficult for them to survive if they did not offload every year a part of those who live there by trafficking slaves". You're all heart, Gerard.

The bourgeoisie then remodelled the city to their refined tastes with the financial backdrop of the slave trade. Whichever way you dress it up, it's all a bit fucked, let's be honest.

So as not to put you to sleep too quickly, I'll save some more of the history for chapter five.

When I arrive, I head off to take a look at a couple of sights before lunch and head firstly for the Chateau.

The Chateau is easy to reach, as it is just a short walk from Gare de Nantes down Boulevard de Stalingrad, which then joins Cours John Kennedy, and unless you have gone in completely the wrong direction, you should see it to your right. To be honest it is pretty hard to miss. It is a strange castle to say the least, the exterior is pretty much as you would expect, large moat, tall and forbidding walls, but inside it is far more refined and has very much a renaissance feel to it, well sort of; or, rather, some of it has. There is a large building, which seems totally out of place called the Batiment du Harnachement. It's a reminder that the castle was also used as an army camp up to the beginning of the 20th century and was home to a lot of ammunition. This is one of the reasons the castle looks so disjointed, as in 1800 the army managed to blow up a large part of the castle by accident.

Anne of Brittany was born here and as previously mentioned, watched over a lot of the construction of what you can see today. If exhibitions are your cup of tea some of the buildings in the courtyard have temporary exhibitions, which you may be charged to enter, but the actual courtyard is free. Generous to a fault these Bretons.

On the bus from the airport I noticed an enormous building, which resembled something out of an old movie set in the Midwest. To take a closer look I head away from Nantes' centre to an Island called Beaulieu de Nantes, which is now a barren industrial wasteland, and probably more intriguing for it. The island is lined with mills and warehouses, but barely any people (not at the weekend anyway) and has a very eerie feel to it, especially if you are alone. This is not a place I would recommend to visit at night, although it is probably quite safe, it doesn't feel it as all you can see is concrete and graffiti, most of which is anti French and pro Breton. 'Free Brittany' and 'Welcome to Brittany' are sprayed and painted on the old ice factory, none the less the place has a fantastic post-modernistic feel to it. No doubt some time soon a real estate agent will acquire and develop these broken down swells of delight for next to nothing and sell them on for an enormous profit to the crazy kids with cash who have their finger on the pulse of popular culture. Oh well.

I find the building I have come to see. The Beghin-Say sugar refinery and it appears to be one of the original buildings still in use. It is the colour that sets it apart from everything else in the grey wasteland, its bright blue wooden front elevation jumps out at you, I could probably be forgiven for thinking it was some kind of folly as opposed to a source of industry. It looks like a barn and has huge stamp-framed windows and stands five stories tall. It's worth a look, if only for its eccentricity. Imagine a lady boy version of Dorothy's farm in Kansas. Back to the 'main land', I make my way through Bouffay, as now I find the area familiar and find a Presse to buy some local papers, to read up on the 'derby of Brittany', and a pew in a café.

The info given is extremely descriptive; it starts with the background of the ref (of all people), who is from Toulouse. He has two children and is a salesman in a large supermarket (riveting stuff). The last time he reffed a game for Le Canaris, we won, so fingers crossed. I cannot get over the idea of Uriah Rennie, filling up the tin goods shelves on the night shift at Asda.

The teams are announced at 2.30pm, the gates are opened at 3.30pm and 35,000 are expected due to the amount of Rennais fans making their way from the neighbouring city.

Interestingly, the paper also mentions that due to the amount of complaints from F.C.N.A. supporters about the price of certain tickets, the club are lowering the price of the next home game (v. Lyon) to 15 euros instead of the usual 20. Again the French decide not to take any shit and demand the respect they deserve, and look what happens. They get the result they wanted, I love this place!

The piece also tells of the importance of this game to Brittany, with other clubs from the region becoming pretenders to the throne (Lorient, Guingamp, and Brest), this is and always has been the true Derby of Brittany. The rivalry between the two clubs is not as sour as it used to be but the match is always one of the tightest competed in the league and there is never a one sided match. The article believes that Rennes will play defensively, while Nantes will go on the attack; as is the preferred tactic of Loic Amisse and the good news is that

Rennes haven't beaten Le Canaris in Nantes for 39 years! For the last five seasons Nantes have won all of the Breton derbies against Rennes and it looks like this trend will continue.

One problem though, for Nantes anyhow, is the long list of injuries the team has. Landreau, the captain, may not play, and the winger, Da Rocha, is also doubtful, plus Berson the aggressive central midfielder is suspended as well. Luckily for them I have my shirt with me.

But the manager has not had many problems selecting a team, with many younger players coming in such as Hadjadj who plays in the centre.

There are also some quips from the Nantes players. Ziani, who has played for both clubs asks, 'What is the true capital of Brittany?' (I don't know Ziani, you tell me).

Vahirua the tiny forward says, 'This rivalry goes beyond sport, it is an historic and economic battle as well'.

Pujol says, ' Nantes and Rennes, from the under 19s to the first team, this is a match like no other'.

Ziani continues, 'Rennes have always been chasing the tails of Nantes but have never reached the same heights and despite the Rennes chairman and his financial means the results have never been as good as they should have been. It is nice to know in football it is not just a question of putting in large sums of money.' Try telling Real Madrid that one.

Oliver Quint finishes the snippets, 'We need to prolong our invincibility at home, it would not be great to be part of the Nantais team that ended the unbeaten record.'

The Rennes manager is, of course, not too interested in the history of not beating Nantes in Pays de la Loire since 1964, and has asked them to play simple football and to enjoy themselves, I'm sure he really means it too. Rennes boast one of the best defensive units in the league and will be hard work for the F.C.N.A. forwards; Vahirua and Pujol, to break down; so they will have to take each chance clinically.

I head for the stadium early to soak up some of the rival atmosphere, and to get a bite to eat. As expected, the place is swarming with both Nantes and Rennes fans and they seem to mingle freely, without too much trouble. Only now and then do I see some riot police leg it where something must have kicked off but these are minor disturbances and don't seem to cause too much hostility with the majority of fans.

I grab a couple of merguez and a 1664. After a nosh and a swig, I take a seat on a bench and do a bit of people watching. Out of the blue this bloke walks up to me and asks me for something, I have no idea what, and tell him I am English (not usually the wisest thing to do at a foreign football match I know, but it just came out). In broken English he asks, 'Are you for Nantes or Rennes?' Even if I were for Rennes, I would have said Nantes as I noticed he was wearing a scarf wrapped around his face with the words 'Brigade Loire' stitched across it. The Brigade Loire is the largest 'Ultra' group at Nantes, and not to be messed with so I am told.

So I tell him I am for Nantes, and I show him my season ticket. He seems bowled over, I go through the motions about coming to the home games from London et al, and he salutes me.

I also tell him I am hoping to write a book about my experiences and would it be possible to stand with the Brigade Loire for a couple of games?

He tells me of course, 'but only if you write about the Brigade' and that he and his friends get free copies. How can I refuse?

I won't name the said Brigade member with his real name, so I will refer to him as X.

X and I enjoy a couple of beers and try to break through the communication barriers, which I seriously have to work on when I get home.

Two Rennes fans walk towards us and X saunters straight up to them and says something. As the Rennais walk off pretty miffed I can only guess it wasn't if they would like to join us for a beer. Just in case I didn't get it the first time around, X puts his arms around me then points to the dejected Rennes fans and screams 'Fuck you', laughs and pats me on the back. Oh dear, I could get into trouble with my new friend.

We exchange mobile numbers in case we get split up on the way into the ground, which it turns we don't as X waits patiently for me as I slow him down as he clambers over seats, around flags and over

people (his shortcut) to get us bang behind the goal. The front row
with his beloved Brigade. Now this lot are a sight more boisterous
than the grannies on the top row in the Jules Verne stand and they
make a fuck of a racket. A young guy, wrapped in a Brigade Loire
scarf, climbs a steel podium at the front and is thrown a megaphone.
Ah so he is our leader.

X tells me to follow his moves when the leader screams the orders.
And it starts, he bellows out something and the brigade raise the flags,
supporting F.C.N.A. will never be the same again.

It is electric, an atmosphere perfect for a derby.

The Nantes anthem blares out, and we all link arms and jump up and
down on the spot singing (when translated literally, it's a little strange)
'He who is not jumping is not for Nantes'. Classic stuff.

The teams come out to immense cheers from both ends and the Rennes
fans set off flares and are booed by their counterparts. X and the
entourage try to get past security, although they probably knew they
wouldn't be able to. The effort is gallant none the less, to make the
Rennais pay for teasing. Instead they are restricted to screaming in
unison 'Rennais, Rennais, fuck you, fuck you' while again jumping up
and down on the spot. I must say this is a fantastic way to keep fit, I
think, while puffing on my umpteenth Marlboro.

My biggest problem is that I see so little of the game that I can barely
report it. The flags are very impressive but I can't see a fucking thing.
I try to dodge the mosh pit as fellow Nantes fans jump on top of each
other but I am thrown wherever they decide to move next.

But one thing is certain, the press was absolutely correct in proposing
that Rennes would stick to their guns and that the defence would be a
bit of a mare to break down. Vahirua and Pujol again and again are
denied glory and all of Ziani's magic is for nothing as his weaving
passes are pounced upon by the Rennes defenders.

22 minutes in though their luck falls to pieces and the young Hadjadj,
who is only playing because of the injuries to so many others, receives
the ball 30 metres out, and the rest happens in slow motion. He
controls it and strikes it cleaner than I have seen anybody strike a ball
under this amount of pressure, probably a lot cleaner than he imagined

he could as well, it screams into the net past the Rennes keeper, Cech. 1-0.

The Loire end erupts into madness, as we jump on top of each other. I'm so pleased for Hadjadj, his first goal, and what a beauty. Only in the team because of absentees and he has taken his opportunity by the horns.

'Allez, allez, allez, allez Nantes, allez', this ditty goes on and on until half time, when they break into 'Allez Nantes' to the tune of Yellow submarine.

The second half pales into insignificance, which is helpful, as it was even harder to see than the first half, especially when the Mexican wave soared around the ground. Of course, I joined in, but I thought this was a little premature and tempting fate. I, for one, didn't want to be part of the crowd raising my arms in joy and unison, when Rennes clawed back an equaliser. Luckily, for the team and the fans, they didn't and another three points were in the bag. Rennes would have to wait a little longer to end their truly abysmal record against the mighty yellows, and, if football is anything to go by, then Nantes is the true capital of Brittany.

After the game I bid farewell to X and his friends and agree to meet X in the same place next time, X marks the spot, ho ho ho (forgive me I'm tired).

I get a cab to meet Hetty's sister, Georgia, at an exhibition one of her chums is having at a gallery called 'Ipso Facto' on Bd. St Aignan. Again, I don't get to see the main event (the artwork), as I can't get in the door due to the amount of people there. So I take advantage of the free wine outside with Georgia and a few of her friends. One of these friends, Fred is a top geezer, with the biggest smile and the biggest hair you will ever see in Nantes. I met him a year or so back, when Georgia had a load of Frenchy buddies over and put on an exhibition in southeast London. We got very pissed together and discovered we shared a major passion for something, which was extremely important to us both, The Smiths and New Order. We sang 'Bizarre Love Triangle', until it was turned off by some evil nemesis from the same party we had attended.

After this exhibition it's off to another one at a gallery called Zoo, located on Chausee de la Madeline. At this one though, there is a D.J. and people who seem to want to talk to me about football, which is always nice. I meet a Bordeaux fan who is very friendly and seems nice but obviously can't be because he's a Bordeaux fan.

I end up getting sloshed and can't remember how I get home. I wake with, yes, yes, yes, a hangover. Fred and Georgia take me for a crepe at Creperie L'Hermine on rue de la Juiverie in the Bouffay area. I go for a Nordique, which is cream and salmon, and is bloody good too. This place is highly recommended by me, plus it is listed in a publication detailing the best pancake houses in Brittany, so if you won't listen to me, listen to them.

5

History continued.
The Champions Ride into Town

The Revolution

Nantes straight away embraced the revolution. Brittany was a province that was in favour of slavery but at the same time was open to the views of the philosophers.

Apart from the views on slavery, the Nantes revolutionaries were dead set against Paris. The hunting down of priests was organised quicker in Nantes than any other part of France.

In 1793, the Montagnards took control of Paris and in Nantes the Girondins maintained the hold on the town hall. So in the eyes of the Parisians, Nantes was not to be trusted. The royalist army went from strength to strength and in the month of June 1793, it was sent to Nantes to, basically, sort them out. They had no idea of what was in store for them…

The royalists outnumbered the Nantais hopelessly but ten thousand men defended the town to the hilt.

This incredible victory for the Republic was named as a 'Valmy in the West', in reference to the town where the Prussians were defeated less than a year before.

Despite this unprecedented victory the Montagnards continued to cast a distrusting eye on Nantes. They sent so-called missionaries to become the sole masters of the city. Carrier was the man charged with the job of sorting out this little problem. In true megalomaniac style, he terrorised the city during what was quite a short mission (October 1793 to February 1794). Carrier enlisted some local revolutionaries and through them he had hundreds of suspects shot and guillotined. At night the Loire barges, crammed with prisoners, were sunk to drown them, as the prisons were already crammed to the max.

Nantes crawled away from the Revolution (and the Napoleonic wars) battered indeed and entered the 19th century with a few steps backwards as the city returned to a familiar tread, moving back into the hugely profitable but now outlawed industry of the slave trade.

The Industrial Port

In the 1800's, the onset railways resulted in maritime trade taking more of a back seat. The opening of the nearby St-Nazaire harbour marked the end of a significant era for the port of Nantes.
So industry would become paramount over trade and in the second half of the 18th century the Lower Loire area built a quarter of all boats in France.
The king of the canning industry, Nicolas Appert joined arms with the confectioner Joseph Colin and begun a new industry which would later feature illustrious dynasties such as Amieux, Cassegrain and Saupiquet. Lois Lefevre-Utile invented his biscuit, the petit-beurre.
The forging mills of Basse-Indre made tinplate cans that were needed to preserve sardines in oil. These are just some of the examples of the business activity, which made sure that Nantes did not miss out on the industrial revolution.

From Then to Now

The First World War took its toll, as it did on most of France, not because of the battle itself, as it was a long way from the front, but because of the call up. More than seven thousand Nantais were killed. Between the wars, Nantes was changed for good. The city that was born unto the water decided to rid itself of the nickname 'the Venice of the west'.
Parts of the Loire were filled in, most prominent of these parts are now in the centre of town, Il Feydeau and Ile Gloriette.
In 1941, one of the directors of this huge construction was shot dead by a member of the Communist resistance. This would be one of the first violent acts against the Germans by the resistance. Needless to say the SS retaliated without mercy. They gathered forty-eight hostages and shot them all. Many of the dead were communists.

This, along with other acts of bravery, resulted in Nantes being one of the few towns to be named Compagnon de la Liberation.

In London on the 11th of November 1941, General de Gaulle said of the City, "as a heroic town, which since capitulation, has put up bitter resistance to all forms of collaboration with the enemy. Through numerous individual and collective acts, it has been a magnificent example to the French of courage and loyalty".

If all the previous death was not enough for this small, yet poignant City, more was to come, this time from the Americans. On the 16th of September 1943 the American air force bombed both the centre of the town and its harbour, which was doubly tragic due to the fact that the Nantais had become sloppy with regard to the air raids. Too many times there had been false alarms so many of the population did not seek refuge in any shelters. Almost fifteen hundred were killed and thousands of buildings were destroyed.

With the disappearance of the shipyards, the exile of the ports, the delocalisation of the canning industry, the fading out of the working class, Nantes had turned its back on one and a half centuries of manufacturing.

Two out of three firms in Nantes today are less than twenty years old. The city now holds half a million in population and is France's seventh largest city, and its population can only conceive of its future as European.

The game after the victory in the Breton derby was away to Metz, again F.C.N.A. were victorious, winning the match 3-1. This put us in the giddy position of fourth in the league.

At Gatwick airport I picked up World Soccer magazine and flicked through, looking for the French league monthly news. Between chomps of some over-priced gunk called an all day breakfast at Garbunkles I read on. The magazine had decided that the rise and rise of Le Canaris was not the most important thing happening in the season so far, instead it concentrated on the row over Monaco and their legitimacy in still being in the French league. Monaco, at the end of last season were broke; and, strictly speaking, should have been relegated due to insufficient funds, as is the custom in the French league. Marseille suffered such trauma on two occasions; of course there was also the small matter of a man called Bernard Tapie and a whole lot of corruption, which was also the deciding factor in this case.

The chairman of Nantes' upcoming opponents Lyon basically argued that the rules have to apply to everyone or the system does not work, that Monaco are not a legitimate football club if they do not follow the rules that the others are forced to.

Fair enough really but on reading about this at the end of last season I knew for certain that there was no way in Hell that A.S. Monaco would be relegated.

The biggest joke about the whole thing now is that, although the financial questions have not all been answered, Monaco have taken on loan Fernando Morientes from Real Madrid, arguably now the biggest name in the league. I can't imagine how they could afford such a player?

The principality of Monaco may have come to the rescue?

This argument, I'm sure will arise again during the season as Monaco look like the only true threat to Lyon's crown.

As things stand at the moment Monaco are top and Lyon are fifth (below us) but I doubt very much that this will be the story at the end of the season as Lyon really haven't moved into top gear yet, and hopefully they won't tonight either.

So the standings are as such –

	Points	Played
MONACO	23	10
MARSEILLE	21	10
P.S.G.	19	10
F.C.N.A.	19	10
LYON	18	10
STRASBOURG	17	10
NICE	16	10
BASTIA	16	10
AUXERRE	14	10
SOCHAUX	14	10
RENNES	13	10
LILLE	13	10
LENS	13	10
MONPELLIER	12	10
METZ	11	10
BORDEAUX	11	10
AJACCIO	11	10

TOULOUSE	9	10
GUINGAMP	5	10
LE MANS	3	10

Already the league is taking shape, with only Bordeaux and Lens of the 'bigger' clubs in the lower part of the division.

Once on the plane, the stewardess passes out free copies of the French daily papers, I take L'Equipe, as it is the only one I can really make any sense out of, plus I can always get someone to translate the parts I don't get.

L'Equipe had compiled a list of how many season ticket holders each club has, like on my previous trip when they did the same kind of report on sponsorship.

Nantes' stadium holds 38,000 and of these 19,031 are abonnes (season ticket holders) that is 49%.

Lyon's ground is a little bigger; 41,000, of these 22,499 are season ticket holders; or 54%.

Lens a notoriously mad football city has a stadium that holds 41,000 and they have 23,749 season ticket holders, a very impressive 57%.

P.S.G. play at the Parc de Princes, which holds 50,000 and they have 18,720 season ticket holders.

Marseille, of course come out on top with a stadium holding 60,000 and 44,253 season ticket holders, a staggering 74%.

I don't know about you, but I'm a bugger for statistics like these. I spend 64.2% of my time trying to work out what I do with the other 35.8%.

The paper devotes quite a bit of space to tonight's game with a headline that is roughly translated as 'Can Nantes mix it with the big boys?' Then there is a yes and a no argument.

Nantes have not had as good a start to the season since the 94-95 season, in which they went on to win the championship, finishing eight points clear of tonight's opponents Lyon; in that season they were unbeaten in 32 matches.

But, although this current crop of players cannot match that of the squad of 94-95, it is still a fantastic start, and it is with great importance that we don't get too carried away because they are yet to play any of the top teams, except Marseille.

The picture will become a lot clearer over the next month or so when they play Lyon, P.S.G. and Monaco.

With only six goals conceded, Nantes have, along with rivals Rennes, the best defensive record in the league. So it is clear where Le Canaris' strength lies at the moment, Landreau is without doubt an international class keeper and the centre back Yepes is the complete defender.

These are the factors that have kept them unbeaten at home until now. In fact the whole defence, as a unit, has been quite formidable so far, and this is a little of a surprise, as Yepes' partner at the back; Gillet and the Argentine full back, Cetto, have been injured now for quite a while.

The problem now though is that Landreau is injured and looking at the fixture list it couldn't have happened at a worse time with so many big teams coming to the Beaujoire. He will be replaced by the second string keeper Wily Grondin, who is respected but is not a touch on the captain.

The left back Armand seems to think that if Nantes can get a goal they should be able to win the game due to the frugality of the defence.

This only worries me, as something like that betrays the fact that there isn't too much faith in the forward line. Pujol is the tall target man but seems a little young to have so much responsibility weighed upon his shoulders.

Vahirua is a proven goal scorer but is so small that in the air you can forget about it ever happening and the service from Pujol is not always great as his first-time touch can let him down.

The play making for the team seems to lay with Ziani and Da Rocha but mainly with little Ziani, if he gets injured, it could be disastrous.

Nantes has one of the youngest squads in the league and the substitute bench is full of enthusiasm but very little experience. But Loic Amisse still seems to be throwing them on, letting them gain experience bit by bit. My only problem with this is that they are too young for such big matches but if there isn't any other fodder for the cannons he will have to make do with what he has.

Out of all the kids the most exciting seems to be Hajadj, who scored that screamer against Rennes and if Nantes carry on as they have been, I reckon we will see a lot more of this chap.

The best the club can hope for is a place in Europe and it says in the L'Equipe article this is exactly what they are aiming for and always have been, so we the supporters shouldn't really hope for too much more. Oh.

Touching down in the former Venice of the west I head to Commerce the busiest part of central Nantes, home to the Gaumont multiplex cinema and a range of shops and eateries, e.t.c.

I go to meet Hetty's sister, Georgia, who is working in a jewellery shop in a place called the Passage de Pommeraye. The Passage is a shopping arcade of the most elegant kind on two levels that links Rue de la Fosse to Rue Crebillon, which is one of the main shopping streets in the city.

Kisses and pleasantries out of the way, we head off for lunch. This makes sense, I have been in France for roughly twenty-five minutes and it's time to eat.

Back to Rue de la Fosse to a restaurant/café called La Trinqette. The food is unsurprisingly excellent and very hearty; a pork stew.

We catch up and I inform Georgia of the family gossip from the past week or so.

After lunch, I arrange to meet her and her boyfriend David in the John McByrne pub.

But before I have to head off to the stadium, I want to take a look at some more of what the city has to offer.

The Stade de la Beaujoire is Nantes' second stadium. The first, the Marcel Saupin, is located behind gare de Nantes.

As far as I am concerned, stadiums, be it for football or for any sports are the greatest of all architectural triumphs.

The years of work in preparation and then building something so huge and wonderful warms me, because although what generally goes on inside the stadia makes revenue, they are not solely built for cash.

Yes, you normally have to pay to enter them and the revenue made by thousands of like minded people keeps them running and therefore gives revenue to the association that either owns them or displays at them, but it is still ours and built for us.

Otherwise pay per view would have been a far bigger success than it has been, the stadia would be empty and we would all just sit 'Strange Days' style and jack in from home to watch the game.

The idea of a stadium proposal landing on an architect's desk must make them want to cum because it is a chance to build a useful folly. 'Design something as wanky and as daring as you see fit as long as it seats X amount of people, X amount of pie stands and X amount of exec boxes for the minted businessmen and stay within budget'. Done.

The Marcel Saupin is far from wanky or daring. It is a two tier, rounded square of a stadium. It's knackered, with smashed windows and graffiti on it and looks like it is about to fall into the Loire from the riverbank it stands on.

Walking around its fractured exterior, I plonk myself down to try and think of the glories this redundant dinosaur must have played host to. Although no longer the first team stadium it does play host to the reserve team and also, so I am told, to rugby games.

I remember Jean-Claude (Xavier's father) reminiscing about the great matches he saw here between what were France's two greatest clubs at the time, Nantes and St. Etienne. He would sit in the upper tier and when the fans really got going the stadium would shake as if it was about to fall down, looking at it now I don't doubt a word of it.

The saddest thing when a club moves from one stadium to the other is the wreckage that it leaves behind it. The cafes around the Marcel Saupin are also relics and stale memorabilia of times passed. Once these match day institutions would be rammed to the hilt and now all that is left over are the locals in these bars whose capacities could never be reached again and photos of previous triumphs of F.C.N.A. hanging sadly from the walls.

Christ, is this what is going to happen to Highbury? Will the Gunners pub and the Highbury Barn really feel like this in ten year's time? Probably.

I leave the forgotten world behind and make my way to Stade de la Beaujoire. It's hard to feel sad about the Saupin when you see this ground as it shows how far this provincial club has come in such a short time and with such limited resources, counting on a youth system that is second only to the remarkable one at Auxerre.

Nantes, I suppose, are a selling club, but with a little bit of a difference. And I think the difference is that they happen to be French or rather they play in the French league.

In the Italian league you have successful clubs that also rely on selling their main assets or in the end let their best players go because they simply cannot afford to turn down the kind of money that a bigger team will offer such as Udinese, Brescia and Chievo. In England, Charlton, Southampton and Bolton would be of similar vein. In Spain Celta Vigo and Espanyol are just a couple of examples.

These are not small clubs by any means but they cannot afford to hold onto outstanding talent for long periods of time if that player wants to leave and if another club (normally with more money or stature) wants them.

But how many of the previously mentioned clubs has won the league in the past ten or fifteen years? None is, of course, the answer, and for this the French domestic league remains unique. It is a far more open form of competition when compared to its European counterparts, saying that though the recent domination by Lyon looks to remain for a while. I can only think of one other league; Russia's, which is close and that has only happened really in the past two seasons when Spartak Moscow have relinquished their stranglehold over the title to fellow Muscovites; Lokomotiv.

France has seen in the past ten years Bordeaux, Lens and Nantes (twice) wrestle away the coveted crown from the big boys from Paris, Marseilles, Monaco and Lyon.

Obviously there is not the same amount of money involved but the competition from other clubs such as the aforementioned and teams like Auxerre (where the incredible forty two year management of Guy Roux has taken them from the province leagues of Burgundy to the heady heights of the first division) makes it a wholly refreshing footballing experience.

Tonight we will see one of Nantes' favourite sons return for a fight with his old teammates. Eric Carrier was one of the most influential in the last title winning side, a central midfielder who can read the game as well as anybody in the league. It seems Nantes knew they would have to resign themselves to losing him but not so quickly (he jumped ship as soon as they won the league) and not to an enemy on home shores either. But alas, he decided to continue to ply his trade in France and for the current champions Lyon.

I wait outside the entrance to the Loire tribune, just in case X pops by. I remember from two weeks ago that he went into the stadium at the last possible moment.

After about five minutes he wanders past. 'X', I exclaim. X turns his head, 'Simon, how arrrrr uuuuuu?'.

I say 'very well, thanks' and return the question. He seems a lot more distant than the last time we met.

It turns out he seems to have the slight hump with me because I said I would call him for information on the Brigade Loire last week.

I apologised and pretend that I lost his number; it would be a lot easier to explain this than the truth you see. What had actually happened was the very uninteresting business of not being able to see my friend Laurie who is French and was going to speak to X directly over the phone for me as my French is crap and X's English is only slightly more refined.

Still we walk into the stadium together and go to the front, behind the goal, assuming the positions with the Brigade. A couple of moody faces recognise me from the last game and nod in my direction, I try to look mean, moody and French and nod back.

Looking at the team sheet, the disappointment is that Landreau is out with injury and is replaced by Wily Grondin, which is a real pity.

The game kicks off at a grindingly steady pace. Nantes are passing well but, again, look a little lost when they cross the halfway line. Lyon look, from where I'm standing, to be playing a 4-3-2-1 formation and, sadly, Elber doesn't seem to be starting today. Nantes are playing a 3-4-1-2 formation, Vahirua and Pujol, are again, the forwards, with Ziani in the pocket just behind them. In midfield Da Rocha, Fae, Berson (today's captain) Armand (playing more wingback than his preferred left back) with Yepes, Delhommeau and Savinaud as the backs in front of Grondin.

Unfortunately, after a small amount of time Nantes look to be slightly (only slightly) out of their depth playing the champions. The sheer patience of Lyon's game when playing away is infuriating for the opposition's players and fans. Not really breaking Nantes down at all, but waiting to wear them out like Ali did with Foreman in the rumble in the jungle, keeping their backs on the ropes. In the last ten minutes of the second half, things begin to change a little. Lyon seemed properly under the cosh and Nantes looked dangerous, especially with bursts of pace from Armand.

In the second half Lyon continued to soak up pressure from le Canaris, only now and again did they seem nervous. They were now playing extremely intelligent football, waiting to move on the break.

Some bad news came about twenty minutes in; the stalwart Columbian, Yepes, got booked and will now miss the P.S.G. game in a fortnight. But, after being booked with his normal heavy gum chewing, bearded stare of hatred at the referee, he turned to the Loire end crowd and raised his hands willing us on to give more bite and enthusiasm to feed the team.

I started to get worried that Yepes would now slow down on his amazing successful tackling ratio but I needn't have worried, he is so competitive that you would probably be more scared to play alongside him than against him in case you did anything wrong.

But five minutes after the booking, Juninho scores, the ball falls to him outside the area and thwack. Back of the net, gutted.

That was that as far as I was concerned. $0 - 0$ would have been a great result but there was no way I thought we would get one back. Twenty minutes to go at 1-0 down with our forwards might as well have been two minutes to go.

I didn't leave the ground but my mind did begin to wander on to other things. About my local college and its French course, which I'm trying to get on. Now and then my brain would focus but only to see another chance gone to the dogs. Lyon had won and they new it, Carrier the traitor had been removed from the game to save him for the next one, and Elber had been brought in for a freshen up run around in the last ten minutes. Talk about rub your face in it.

So we lost 1-0.

I stayed to listen for the results from around the country, via the tannoy, to hear where we would be in the league.

Ajaccio and P.S.G. had drawn, Montpellier had surprisingly beat Auxerre, Guingamp beat Toulouse, Le Mans and Bastia drew, OM unsurprisingly beat Rennes, Nice and Bordeaux drew, Strasbourg and Metz drew and Lens beat Lille.

So if my maths were up to any sort of form we would have only dropped one place to 5th, which I suppose is not so bad. Lyon have leapfrogged us into fourth place and are now once again in the title race, which it seems will probably be between them and Monaco.

Lyon may be known everywhere else as the champions of French football and the true home of gastronomy but to me Lyon will always be the city that wouldn't let me go for a shit.

I venture to my post match hangout, the John McByrne. Both Dave and Mick are behind the bar, bickering in a jesting kind of vibe. They greet me and serve up some lovely stout, which costs pretty much the same price as admission to one home game at F.C.N.A with an abonne. Still mustn't grumble.

A chap mills around close to me looking a little lonely. I know he is British and not from these parts as he hasn't tucked his shirt into his jeans.

I introduce myself and he turns out to be a truck driver called Bruce from England on a long haul delivery. The reason he was stopping off in Nantes was that around fifteen years ago his friend and he stopped on the outskirts, on a European backpacking tour. They met a couple of girls and Bruce's girl put him up at her family's house and basically bonked his brains out for two weeks solid. 'Two of the most beautiful weeks of my life', he adds, almost needlessly.

Tomorrow he will head off to the satellite town to find her before he sets off on the road again to deliver more crates of goods to the great and the good.

Before I can think of becoming a long distance truck driver I get a slap on the back. I turn around and it's my hosts Georgia and David, along with another friend whom I recognise but cannot remember where from.

The lad's name is Willy and he comes from Ancenis. He is one of David's partners at Clown School. Willy and Dave are professional clowns and teach during the week just outside the city. I am in the company of artists once again in this small cultural cauldron and feel rather capitalist in my vocation as a Marketing Manager of an industrial cleaning company/theatre company.

Willy tells us that a new bar has opened on Feydeau called La Gargouille, which is a rum bar. The place turns out to be quite small and narrow and the interior is made almost completely of wood. The barman welcomes us in with a friendly wave but we are taken aback by the stares we receive from the clientele. This amuses all of us, as we seem to have arrived on under age drinking night and at some schoolchild's birthday party. The place is rammed with juvenile drunken fury, it's like Byker Grove being let loose in a brewery. Well we have made the walk and so decide to sample the tipple this establishment has to offer; the barman seems keen for us to stay and save him from the brats before the place is drowned in vomit. We make our way through some of the hanging rum bottles on offer and take shots each of coconut, ginger, lychee and licorice. Most are grotesque, and yet they seem to call to you, to taste them once more. Before we know it the wooden room is spinning and we can see why our younger cousins have ended up swinging from the ceiling. We make for the door.

David leads us to a personal favourite of his and Willy's called the Blue Note café located at 26, rue de la Rosiere d'Artois. The owner recognises David and seats us at the back of the bar, which is where the table football is situated. Once seated, we are presented with punch, which seems the pride of the bar and on top of the rum makes my guts feel like a washing machine on rapid-wash cycle. We play a game of table football, David and I pair up and naturally thrash the clown and woman partnership playing opposite us. The owner then brings us caramel vodka, I wonder if anybody around here has heard of beer. The vodka is equally violent on my insides and tomorrow's urine will be a punch in itself.

Next stop kebab shop. Again I witness the difference in French and English junk food and it's not simply that I'm not accustomed to the Franco-kebab. The quality in all food whether it from a café, restaurant or a kebab shop is simply superior. Georgia wants to go home and I can't say I disagree what with the mixture being digested in my stomach. But David and Willy have the taste and we move on to another of their faves.

'Live Act' is the name, a little strange as we enter into the two-floor bar/disco as the only music being played was pre-recorded by a D.J. Again, the staff recognises the trio of Georgia, Dave and Willy and we take seats at the bar. David orders himself and I a Picon, which is a pression (beer from the tap) with a dash of Picon that is, I suppose some kind of fortified wine. David informs me it makes the beer taste softer and easier to drink; he usually has one after a skin full. It may make it taste softer, he's absolutely right, but in fact it turns what was 5% beer into 7.5% and gets you even more pissed.

You may have noticed I didn't put the address of 'Live Act' when I introduced the bar, apologies, but I can't remember where it is, and I can't remember how we got home.

The only way to get over a bad result, the French/Breton way.

6

Here Comes Trouble

The week after the Lyon defeat, Nantes travelled to the south of France to play Montpellier and lost; a humiliating four goals to one, Armand scored for Nantes.

I remember to phone X before my next home game adventure so as not to offend him. He says he will meet me earlier than usual to give me a CD-rom with all the information I could ever need to know about Brigade Loire on it. The main reason he wants to meet early is because the Brigade will be entertaining the Paris ultras and are looking forward to a big fight.

Parisians do not seem to be popular anywhere in the provinces, but even more so in football where they seem hated. The game between Marseille and P.S.G. is called the derby of France.

The ultras that the Brigade Loire want to fight is unclear so I have a look on the P.S.G. website for the names of ultra groups and come up with quite a few. Their names are 'The Authentiks', 'Boulogne Boys', 'Lutece Falco' and 'Supras'. I wonder which of the listed they want to bust up, maybe all of them.

Looking at the last couple of results a draw would be a good result. We are still fifth and the Parisians are just ahead of us in fourth. The top six looks like this:

1	Monaco	27 points
2	Lyon	24 points
3	Marseille	24 points
4	P.S.G.	20 points
5	F.C.N.A.	19 points
6	Lens	19 points

As you can see, if we lose today we could go down further if Lens get a result at home against Montpellier.

On the Gatwick express, at six in the morning, I try to look at some print offs from both the Nantes and P.S.G. websites but everything seems a bit of a blur this morning and I just can't manage it.

During the week I had spoken to a couple of French guys about P.S.G. and although it might seem a little unfair because neither are Parisians they both had some heavy animosity towards the club. Firstly, the reasons were that the club is manufactured and only came about because of the demise of the 'real' football club of the capital, Racing. Secondly, the club's hardcore fan base has long been a breeding ground for fascist-like groups and neo-nazis.

Thirdly, they come from Paris.

There are a lot of clubs that have to carry the stigma of being a 'fascist' club. Lazio and Verona in Italy are regarded as right wing, especially Lazio but it doesn't mean you have to be a right winger to support them. So apologies to P.S.G. fans everywhere that are not extreme right-wingers in their political thinking and simply follow the club because they are Parisians.

Once at the airport I take a look in one of the duty-free sport shops and at the latest kits. It is strange how over the course of a few months a club can become unfashionable to the shirt wearing fan. This is always easier to view in a small sport shop that only sells a few replica kits. This same place used to sell both Lazio and Roma shirts because it was only a couple of years ago that they won the title, each in consecutive seasons. But now they are nowhere to be seen. Real Madrid shirts are everywhere as are Chelsea's shirts and A.C. Milan seems to be back on the front row too after their Champions League final win over Juve.

The plane lands at Aeroport Nantes Atlantique and I pass through customs and am stopped and searched. The customs officer asks what I am doing in Nantes and I say 'I am here for the football, I'm English. I watch the matches here in Nantes'.

'Oh, you are a footballer?' he replies.

'No, I am journalist' I lie. But again it seems so much easier and believable than the truth, just like when I lied to X at the Lyon game.

He waves me on slightly disappointed it seems but at the grand age of twenty-seven I have become accustomed to disappointing people around me.

The Tan air shuttle bus to Commerce is waiting outside; I either just seem to get it when coming off the plane or I miss it and wait for three quarters of an hour. I am in luck this time and I take it as omen for the game this evening. A girl gets on the bus and sits opposite me and asks me something in a very strong southern French accent that I can't understand. She finds out I'm English and we natter for a while. She is from St. Tropez and very trendily dressed, possibly a little too racy for the smartly dressed Nantais who sit and stare at us as the bus zooms towards the city. She is here for a friend's birthday as a surprise and asks me if I would like to come. I say 'Sorry I'll have to pass as I have flown over to watch the game'. She smiles, disappointed, I think and I feel flattered and rather ashamed as I used football as an excuse and not Hetty my girlfriend who I am about to ask to marry me to forgo her invitation to revelry.

I have arranged to meet Georgia at a café/bistro called the Café du Passage, which is located on Rue St. Pierre opposite the huge church, which I have still yet to investigate.

She is in jovial mood and once again it seems that she has decided not to sleep and party all night. We tuck into lunch rapidly as she has to head back to work. I ask her a favour, to call X. I tell her to tell him that I won't be at the game until later as my plane is delayed. I really don't fancy a fight to be honest.

It is good news, X is not worried and will either see me during the game or after, near the beer tents.

Result.

After lunch we head back to the Passage Pommeraye where Georgia is working in 'Passage 31' the jewellery shop. I am here to look at engagement rings and one catches my eye but it just seems rather too bulbous to expect Hetty to wear that for the rest of her life, which is a pity as it's beautiful and only half the price of others I have seen.

Gutted.

Instead of heading to the stadium early for a fight I head to 'La Perle' a fantastic dive bar that shows football on TV. 'La Perle' is located between Passage de Pommeraye and Commerce down a small alley and has a kebab shop next door. The owner of the bar is the friendliest I have met in Nantes and makes you feel very welcome in what, otherwise, would seem extremely hostile territory (to the naked eye anyway).

Flanked around the loud and talkative leader are his adoring children who are unbelievably well behaved and his mates who just keep on coming in, normally with a kebab from next door. Football, Pastis and beer is the order of the day in this place. Oh, and gambling. There is racing news all over the place as well as F.C.N.A. posters and fixture lists and newspapers are folded firmly to the back page for racing news. Every now and again one of the blokes grabs the phone at the end of the bar and rushes a bet on. Then the owner flicks the football over momentarily to watch the race. 'Only one minute' he says smiling at me. What a dude.

He needn't worry too much; the game is Wolves versus Birmingham. But they seem entertained, as every time the Brummies get the ball there are shouts of 'Dugarry'!

Back to the Black Country derby and I'm bored shitless. Even a maniac football fan can be bored by his blessed game. Christ's teeth! Did any of these players watch football when they were kids, they may as well piss off now and call it a draw and save themselves some effort and their fans should get their money back at the gate.

It reminds me that the fans of the clubs playing on the TV via satellite link up to ol' blighty probably paid in the region of twenty quid plus for a ticket. I'm sitting here on my third beer with a season ticket in my pocket for Nantes and I've only spent £53 pound more and I'm a lot fucking happier, I can tell you. In fact when the kids go home after the match they should turn to their Dad's and say 'being that most of the players who turn out for my chosen football club don't seem to give two shits about me Dad, I've decided that when I grow up I'm going to support a team that plays value for money football. I'm sorry Dad, I'm not a turn coat I've just had enough of being stung…Goodbye Daddy and thanks for trying'.

I don't stay for the end of the game and I think the locals were quite pleased because I'd only just put on my coat and the channel was changed back to horse racing.

I walk out of the bar and there seems to be a bit of an invasion from the capital. The streets are full of the blue and red of P.S.G. It all seems good-natured. The same as you see anywhere when travelling fans descend upon a town. As far as they are concerned they have come, seen and conquered. To me that kind of shit is a joy to watch. They barge around, with a strength in numbers kind of vibe going on. Women move their children out of the way with a small amount of fear, then the fans that they have sheltered their nearest and dearest from move up to the kids and rub them on the head or wink at them. It's beautiful shit, baby!

They are a boisterous bunch, to say the least. The chic boutiques of Passage de Pommeraye look on in astonishment, then they realise they are football fans and it's all okay. Paris St. Germain chants are offskies ahoy and I must admit I take off my Nantes baseball cap just in case of trouble.

I make my way through the crowd down to Bouffay to visit my local, the John McByrne. Brummie Dave the barman (Villa), is my side of the bar for a change and greets me enthusiastically. I now seem to be regular and the locals and bar staff have taken me under their wing. Mick is behind the bar and in his usual grumpy-on-purpose-to-get-a-few-laughs kind of mood, and, to be fair, his act always works, on me anyway. Dave is being entertained by a maddish fellow that I will name the 'Magic man' because it is my book and I can. Magic Man is doing some funky tricks and Dave, who doesn't seem totally off his head, seems mightily impressed by the goings on.

Magic Man asks various things of various people near to him and does some 'miraculous' tricks and everyone is gob smacked for three seconds then we all start talking and drinking again. I don't mean to sound cynical but you know the score, come on yes you do. Oh come on, I'm not a complete cunt!

Suddenly the door flies open and the place is full of P.S.G. fans and Dave the barman cheers.

'What the fuck is wrong with you, they're P.S.G.' I rant in his face.
'I lived in Paris for three years before I came here. Allez P.S.G'.
Wanker, you think you know somebody, then...

One of the P.S.G. fans gives him a scarf and he starts work behind the bar with it on.

I feel pure anger at him. I admit I've had a few but all the same, don't piss down my back and tell me it's raining. Don't shit on your own doorstep, don't play hide the fudge with the hide the fudge European champion. Sorry it's all a bit much.

Another guy called Simon (Notts Forest) is chilling out with a couple of mates and we get chatting, he seems a pretty good guy and we buy each other a beer while talking about football.

By this time the place is over run with the capital's representatives, including all the outside seating area.

Magic Man is making his rounds and his tricks for drinks seems to be a right royal success being that he's half cut. His latest victim is mightily impressed and he turns to me and asks me if I want a drink. I give him the obvious answer and we introduce ourselves. His name is Cederic and he is here for the match as well but he is a supporter of the other team.

He tells me of his affiliation with the club but he doesn't actually support them. He was brought up in Paris, but by Breton parents and he feels in himself that he is Breton, but at the same time he is very proud to be French. The only reason he watches P.S.G. is because they are his nearest team and he simply loves watching football. He carries on telling me he came with a crew and that they are his friends but at the same time they are not.

I ask him to explain what he means and then the dreaded right wing issue raises its ugly head. 'They boo black players. They are totally racist; I'm not a racist. If one of our black players gets the ball or scores he is a champion, if the opposition's black players touch the ball they get vilified' he explains.

'Don't you find it difficult to support a football club like that, where the hardcore fans are renowned for their racist abuse of players and their right wing views?'

He continues 'I have a problem with racism but I am proud to be French, so I am right wing. Marseille are the left to P.S.G. As far as the ultras are concerned they are all African and I must admit when they burn the French flag at the derby I just feel hatred towards them.' I ask Cederic what he thinks of F.C.N.A.

' Nantes are a sound football club, they play good football with players they have mostly raised themselves which is what I believe football should be all about. Grass roots. At P.S.G. there are too many skin heads, it can get quite ugly, sometimes it's not about football for the ultras.'

'Do you think there will be a fight tonight?' Knowing full well there is an ambush being organised by X and Co.

'Of course, always away from home'.

We sit for a while and sup our beers, not talking, I mull over what Cederic has been saying and I really don't know what to think. Some of the things he has said are entirely valid and he seems like a very intelligent guy but I can't help thinking that if you were a direct witness to racist views, views which you didn't believe in, surely you would travel with some other fans. I don't believe for one second that all of his mates who like football are racist.

Our heads swing round as we hear a commotion outside, a Rasta walks past one of the tables. There are some things said as he strides past, he turns and says something back. Christ, I wish he hadn't, the table got up and followed him and a skinhead glassed him and started kicking the shit out of him before the poor fucker ran away.

Bouffay is a pretty busy place but nobody did a thing, no police were called and people went about their business.

Eventually the table of fans was asked to move on. Cederic finished his pint. 'That's me, I've got to go'.

'You came with them?'

'Yes I'm afraid so, take my phone number, if you come to watch a game in Paris I'll take you out on the town'.

I take his number and watch him leave. Simon of Nottingham takes a seat beside me. 'That's the one thing that gets me here. That kind of shit would not happen at home, we are light years ahead of the French when it comes to shit like that. If an English bloke did that he'd get the shit kicked out of him by blacks and whites' he says.

'In most places, yeah I think you're right. But, we didn't do anything did we?' I reply while trying to count how many times he just said shit.

'They would have murdered us'. And he's probably right. Fuck them I hope they get caned in that fight and sent home to Mummy on Sunday morning with fresh bruises so they get grounded for a month.

On the tram up to Beaujoire I feel pissed, far more than I thought I was and then think back to my first drink of the day at La Perle and l check the current time. It's seven and I've been drinking pretty much constantly for six hours. My Dutch courage is sky high and as the tram is rammed with supporters of Le Canaris I try to start up a song, with my limited French I head for a basic one. 'Allez, Allez Nantes Allez – whoaa, whoaa. Allez, Allez Nantes Allez – whoaa, whoaa' I stand-alone, and if I wasn't so blotto I would have curled up in humiliation, instead I make a total arse of myself and fall over. Christ on a bike, I'm mullered.

I get off the tram the stop before Beaujoire because my bladder is screaming for help. I stumble around looking for a decent bush to siphon the python in but none suffice. I wander up to a largish van and take a pee behind that. It feels rather wonderful to be honest, not quite as wonderful as the giant crap I had in Lyon once Hetty had arrived and paid for it (it's going to haunt me for life, that miserable day), but it ranks pretty close. Then there is a problem. A uniformed policeman stands in front of me once I zip up the snake. I try to explain myself and he just looks at me, I then realise I have pissed on his van and that's why he's a little upset. But as a true European brother he lets me off, once I explain that I'm English. Not many times an Englishman abroad can claim something like that.

I make off, hastily giggling to myself about the previous shenanigans and head towards the bright lights of the stadium.

As Cederic promised there are misdemeanours a go-go outside the ground. I wander towards one of the less busy stalls and get a couple of Merguez and a beer. Once I've scoffed the first one down I watch a few of the fights, which don't seem to be being extinguished as soon as they could be. Then a beer bottle flies over my section of the crowd and smashes near a couple of kids who obviously leg it as soon as. Although there seemed to be quite a large police presence both in the city and here they really don't seem to be doing too much. A lot of them are sitting in their vans and the coppers that are walking around tend to be waiting for something a little bigger to happen before they pull out the batons.

Inevitably it does. Like maddened suicide bombers some P.S.G. fans take it in turns to randomly run at the crowd and start attacking people; although it is a pure act of savagery, it is also pretty amusing because they look like such twats. They kick a couple of people then prance away back to their gatherings and are hidden by their buddies so once the police finally get to the scene of the crime they are having another beer and bragging about the poor fucker they just kicked in the ribs. All right, not amusing really.

One of the suicide bombers gets his comeuppance. He takes on one too many, and gets a bit of a kicking himself. Then the police make it over and drag him by his cheap and nasty bomber jacket (the type you would only be able to find on the continent, or if you had a time machine and pinched one off the set of an early eighties episode of Grange Hill) across the ground and he cuts his back up then for good measure is slung into the back of a police van. Pity, he would have been stimulating conversation at half time.

Suddenly there seems to be some kind of triple suicide bomber pact and they are heading right in my direction. Fuck, shit, piss, run, run, shit, fuck. I leg it (with others mind, they weren't just after me I can assure you of that). They find their victims, start kicking them and then the police head in, batons wielding.

'Simon how arrrr uuuuuuu?' It's X and a few mates that I met two home games ago.

X tells me this is the worst he has ever seen but it is far from over. He doesn't seem to have a scratch on him so maybe the main event battle has been cancelled or simply postponed until after the game, or he chickened out just like me.

We make our way to the front of the Tribune Loire, behind the goal as is becoming customary. X helps me along now and then when he realises just how bad my balance is because of my drink intake. He informs me he has forgotten to put the Brigade info on a cd-rom. The stadium is the busiest I have seen it so far this season and there is a lot of pre-match noise. The P.S.G. fans in the Erdre end are screaming away and setting off flares.

More and more of the Brigade Loire make their way to their usual spots, I begin to recognise faces. It looks to me that maybe the fight has happened after all as they all look in a pretty bad way. Black eyes and cut lips ahoy on the front two rows of the Tribune Loire, man they look a right state. If they won (if anybody wins these types of scraps, or maybe they are just stopped) the P.S.G. fans must look like shit. I don't ask X any questions as he shakes hands with his mauled colleagues just in case they got slaughtered.

The players come out to a massive cheer and the team from the capital get the expected response 'P.S.G. Fuck you' times three, and from the top, times three and chorus, and rest.

In goal again for us tonight is the second string goalkeeper Grondin, so Landreau is still out. This means we are missing three of our top players, as Yepes is suspended and Vahirua is on the bench, Ahamada has replaced him tonight.

P.S.G. play with a straight forward 4-4-2 formation with the ex-Bordeaux, Portuguese forward, Pauleta, up front alongside Fiorese. Paris start the strongest, Pauleta and Fiorese combining well early on and with some slick supply from Boskovic. Pauleta passes the ball out left to Boskovic who gets a good shot on goal but it is forced away by Grondin.

The capital's team kept up their attacking, and for the first twenty minutes have the game by the scruff of the neck. Fiorese has a good effort saved also.

Nantais have to wait for half an hour before anything promising from their team happens. Da Rocha, who is looking better by the game, heads a fierce shot from an Armand cross, but it is well saved by Alonzo.

At half time X does his usual disappearing act (mmm, maybe he doesn't like me) and I am left by myself. But, I scream and sing along to all the Nantes songs, jumping up and down in all the right places, it seems I have got the hang of Le Canaris dance movements.

At the beginning of the second half Nantes play out of their skins. They have four corners in less than ten minutes, but Alonzo, who must surely be the man of the match is formidable in goal and it seems that we will not get past him tonight.

P.S.G. get one true chance and, yes you've guessed it, they score. Fiorese gets a lucky rebound on the edge of the box and twats it across the goal and it beats Grondin. Needless to say the capital's travelling fans go ape-shit and more flares go off.

Then it is over; I'm totally gutted. Against Lyon we might have been more promising in attack than the visitors but Lyon had something, calmness, patience and waited for the right moment.

This case was very different, we outplayed P.S.G. from twenty odd minutes in, right up to the final whistle, they got one shot at goal in the second half and it went in. If it weren't for the form of Alonzo we would have trounced the bastards.

Still, that's football. My last two trips to Nantes have been fruitless when it comes to getting points. This means we drop to sixth and P.S.G. have suddenly made the top three and look like they could have a serious say in where the title will go this year, which is even more bizarre given the way they just played.

I leave the ground totally pissed off; this has been a bit of a nightmare. Maybe it's the amount of drink but this is the most involved I have felt, I began to get the bug proper in the Lyon game, but now it feels like it is here to stay, which right now doesn't feel like the greatest thing in the world.

I sleep in and don't wake until twelve. Georgia wakes me gently; she knows now not to wake me up so early as I am bloody moody in the morning. Today we are going to the botanical gardens.

Although November probably isn't the best time to visit the gardens it is still an inspiration.

Get the tram to Gare de Nantes and walk over the road and you will see a café on your left, keep going straight and you'll see the entrance.

This route is probably the nicest way to go because the noise of the city dies away so quickly as you head through the gardens towards the exit, which will bring you out in the St. Clemente area, not far from the Musee de Beaux Arts.

Nantes' fascination with all things botanical started way back in the days of Louis XV when he signed an order that all sea captains on returning to port bring as many plants and seeds as possible with them. There is a palm house near the Clemente end, which has a very colonial feel to it, in the summer it must be quite majestic, I'll have to come back and take another look then. Another little fact about the gardens is that it is host to the oldest magnolia cultivated in Europe, it is an American tree planted here in 1787. Titchmarsh, you're sacked!

Before I make my way to the Airport, we pop in to see Georgia's friend, Pierre. He has a gift for Hetty and me.

He has just returned from Bolivia and has brought with him some charms made by the locals near the town he was staying in.

The charm is a small medicinal bottle, filled with small painted wooden objects and oils.

In truth it's a little bizarre.

'This is the first one I have given, it is because you are to marry, and it is for luck' he informs me.

I'm taken aback by my new friends gesture. He then tells me 'you must never open it, if you open it you die'.

'Oh' I say feebly. Then I mull over how the hell I am going to get something so weird looking through airport security. I know he did but a Bolivian customs officer or security guard is going to know exactly what it is and not bother to investigate it further. The French, on the other hand may open it at the airport and then I'll know Pierre wasn't fibbing about the consequences of 'messing with' the charm as my plane plummets into the channel.

I needn't have worried, I'm so late that they have held the plane for me and rush me through customs.

I board the plane and feel the glare of the delayed passengers' angry eyes as I sit down and pretend to fall asleep.

7

Homecoming of a Prodigal Son

I gave up on X delivering the required information on the Brigade
Loire and hunted through a variety of web pages on Ultras and in the
end found their website, www.brigadeloire.free.fr
The site is quite impressive and the Brigade must have a couple of
decent designers in their midst to have such a quality site. There are
pages upon pages of photos from different games and loads of
background information. I went to the history page and what follows is
a very rough breakdown of what I think is written there.
In August 1998 the Loire end kop was replaced by seating. This, to a
certain extent, brought an end to the camaraderie that you can only
have on the terraces. So a few Loire end fans started to surf the net to
find other like-minded individuals to form some kind of group, an
ultra group. They were looking for people to form some kind of gang,
so to speak that stood individual from the club and was strictly for the
involvement of fans at the games. Eight guys at first were the core of
what would later become the Brigade Loire.
The group would meet in various places, an Irish pub and the Hotel
Inn in Beaujoire. Here, between many pints of beer they tried to forge
a name for their ensemble. 'Section VIP' and 'the House of Fun' were
the leading lights for a while until they settled upon 'Brigade Loire'. It
was a perfect name as it represented the tribune where they stood and
the word Brigade, an army, like the ultras used in Italy.
Then like any ultra group they started to design flags and banners.
And so…
The Brigade now has in the region of 150 members, which will only
grow, as they seem to be the leading light of fan groups at the
Beaujoire.
Some of the merchandise is pretty funky, they have their own scarves
and some wicked hooded tops, which I suppose along with the scarf is

a great disguise when throwing flares at rival fans while being photographed by the police.

A week before my next trip out to Nantes.

I finished work early to head off to the anti-war march in Trafalgar Square. Along with thousands of others, I welcomed George Bush to London in my own special, little way.

It's hard to remain calm in a situation like so many of us witnessed that day. During the occupation of Iraq by U.S. troops, Tony Blair decides to welcome the leader of the 'free' world to London. Now this would be a normal procedure for any government but it was the way in which it was done and the lack of respect for so many of his countrymen, many of whom voted for him and gave him his second term in office. The man acted like a motherfucker, and even if you were pro-war, you must have been thinking 'bad timing Tony, you've just lost yourself a lot of respect, not to mention voters'.

My old flat-mate, Pat, had made it to the march earlier and I met him as he came up Whitehall to Trafalgar Square. The night went very peacefully, we listened to speeches and some of the computer images flashed up on a massive video-screen in the square were fantastic. The best of these images were a spinning pretzel, in homage to the same bit of snack food that almost choked Georgie boy to death while he was watching some pro-football, down on the ranch. The other image was a tad darker and, depending on your political persuasion, extremely funny. An image of Bush stepping out of his car on a loop, with a sniper sight following his heart in an assassination attempt. Genius.

After the rally Pat and I and some of the Bristol Socialist Workers Party that we had met went to a nearby pub. A couple of drinks turned into a shed load and I wasn't looking forward to work the next morning, so I decided that when I got up the next day I would phone in sick.

We moved on to another bar and then bid our red friends a fond farewell. Now all we had to do was get home to south London. I said to Pat that we should go down to the palace, where Dubya had been tucking into some blighty grub cooked by the devastatingly weird and vacant chef and shagger of ex Tory marketing guru (well one half of anyway), Nigella.

The police presence was obviously large and most of the protesters had dwindled at this late hour, probably due to the heavy rain that was pouring down on us at this moment.

We were drunk but I'm still quite proud of what we did. We waited for the police guard to change over and while most of the filth were in a van, we broke through the barrier and ran at the palace chanting and protesting. Pat went one way around the van and I went another so we wouldn't be caught so quickly (we had already resigned ourselves to the fact that we were not going to win this battle). I almost got hit by a car and skidded across the road on my arse, when I got up I charged to the gates with Pat, screaming general obscenities at W. Before I knew it the gates electronically slammed shut and I was on the floor with my face in a puddle.

I winced open an eye and saw Pat in the same predicament about ten feet away and we both started to laugh. The three policemen on top of each of us were not so amused and yanked us to our feet. I felt an instant stabbing pain near my right shoulder and when they cuffed me it felt fucking awful. I tried to explain to the jolly officer who was ramming my body into the police van that I might have a little problem with the arm, old chum, but it fell on deaf ears and angry eyes.

The trip to Charing Cross nick was quite pleasant as we passed a lot of the major tourist attractions of this fine city, and in such great company too.

Our photos were taken; mine was rather charming as I had the giggles. I tried to control myself but I gave in to fits of laughter. While laughing like a freak I again explained that my arm was rather painful and I may need to see a doctor.

The policeman who must have jumped on me first said 'don't worry about your arm, you should think of my jaw, I smacked it when I jumped on you'.

What a pity. And yes I'm sure I will regularly think of you and your jaw on many occasions in my sad empty life, maybe one day pen a book of my experiences with the Met called 'The Filth and Me...A memoir of the misguided'.

We got separate cells and eventually I was taken to hospital. They had broken my collarbone, and I would have to wait six weeks for it to heel. Funnily enough they didn't charge me and I was free to go, but Pat (whom they broke none of) was charged with being drunk and disorderly and would spend twelve hours inside and go before a judge in the morning.

Madman wasn't best pleased but I was going to phone in sick anyway, at least now I didn't have to lie. Luckily my boss is a good bloke and as left wing as a boss can be, so the thought of me not being able to ride my scooter around doing quotes for his company wasn't the end of the world. Plus a few sick days would be more money in the coffers for him.

After we lost to Paris, Nantes then travelled to Corsica to play Bastia and halted their bad run with a 3-1 win. The Nantes scorers were Vahirua, Fae and Ziani.

Another bit of news, monumental news to the average F.C.N.A. fan, and news that seems to have passed me by; it has passed me by due to my lack of French and the fact the company I hold when in Nantes is not one of football fanatics...

Moldovan has returned! The Romanian striker and God to the Beaujoire faithful left last season to hit the mega money Saudi league (I think it was Saudi). Well it seems he didn't really like it all that much and returned in September. Although he is in Nantes, he is still not a member of the team, probably due to the transfer window, I'm not entirely sure. So it seems that I will have to wait until January to see what the fuss is all about.

Since I have been here he has had a kind of Colonel Kurtz vibe over the whole situation; his presence is felt, but he isn't on show, just like the first three-quarters of Apocalypse Now. When people talk about the club, Viorel Moldovan is often mentioned in the same breath and I was disappointed on my arrival that he was no longer part of the club set up, firstly because I knew who he was and secondly I've seen him play many times, albeit televised and thought he was pretty good.

I get to Nantes with my arm in a sling and everything is a little harder to do than usual, due to my deformity, but hey! I manage because I'm one of the tough guys.

Bit of a poor show from the weather, it is very wet, but a little warmer than the big smoke.

I make my way to Georgia's jewellery shop, pleasantries, blah, blah, blah. Georgia draws me a map to her new apartment that she has started to rent with Dave. I follow the map without any hassle (even with one arm!) and pass through Place de Graslin, home to the opera house and the cities 'finest' restaurant 'La Cigale'.

The flat is very empty and quite possibly the most French looking apartment I've ever been in. Tall windows, shutters, long narrow rooms, it's quite beautiful. There is no furniture either, and this makes me a little nervous as this weekend Dave and Georgia have invited over Pierre (head of arts for the council) and a lady called Dominique, who is the head of communications for Nantes. They are coming to dinner to talk about my book tomorrow. Maybe they can sit on the floor?

Later on a friend of David and Georgia walks in says hello and plonks down some garden furniture. Well there we are, this will do.

I decide for my big night with the council homies that I will pretend I hurt my arm whilst falling off my scooter as this sounds a little less lunatic fringe, so as not to scare them off. My other problem is doing my hair with one hand; it's a real fucker!

And so, here we go again.

France is in the middle of the harvest Beaujolais Nouveaux and the lovely vin is bloody everywhere, not that the average Frenchman likes the tipple too much, claiming that each year it seems to taste even more like banana than the last. I personally love the stuff and try to get as much of it as I can each year and drink myself silly.

Secondly, it's the principality club rolling into town, Monaco. And things seem to be going rather well for the Monegasques and their manager, Didier Deschamps. Deschamps is thought of fondly here in

Nantes, as he was a member of the team that won the league in the nineties along with Karembeu and Desailly.

Deschamps is one bloke in football that I truly respect. At club and international level he has won the lot and here he is now managing; his thirst for the game is still not quenched. He had a difficult time of it last season and many thought that he was straight for the scrap heap. But the club hierarchy at Monaco stuck by him and so they bloody should too. The guy has played for Nantes, Marseilles, Juventus, Chelsea and Valencia, none of which are middle of the road clubs, and he has excelled at most, especially Juventus when he was at his peak. This of course does not make you a great manager but now they are top of the league and scoring freely, the chairman must be truly pleased that he didn't listen to the media or a section of the clubs fan base.

Tonight, this prodigal son returns to the club that nurtured him and made him what he is today, and what does he want to do in return? Beat us. It's funny how things go around.

The team he has assembled and inherited is quite a formidable force. Giuly, the captain, is a great player, a goal scoring, attacking midfielder, Prso and Morientes up front have quickly formed a partnership that is second to none in the league and the other position they are strong in is in goal. Roma turned down a move to Arsenal before the season began, I have no idea why, maybe he prefers not to pay tax, but hey we ended up with Jens Lehman, who is either a genius waiting to happen or just a nutter.

Last season at Beaujoire, Monaco beat us 2-0. If anybody is going to knock Lyon off their perch and stop them winning a third consecutive title it is the southerners. Lyon are at Nantes' archrivals, Rennes tonight, who have a pretty mean defence but whether they have the steel to keep out Lyon is another kettle of fish.

I settle down on the sofa with L'equipe and look through today's witterings and try to make out what I can. It is a bit of kafuffle turning broadsheet newspaper pages when you can only use one arm. I decide I don't want this bloody nuisance of a thing to be around any longer than it needs to be so I don't think I will watch the game with the Brigade tonight, just in the unlikely case that we score and there is a heaving surge to the front of the Loire end. I get bored lying around and head off into the rainy seventh largest city in France and to the Museum Dobree.

The Museum of Thomas Dobree is not your average, run-of-the-mill museum by any means. At first glance the old buildings on rue Voltaire are indeed grand but there is no hint of the treasures that lie in wait.

The place is crammed to the hilt and is basically elaborate bric-a-brac. For many generations the Dobree family had a decisive hand in the status of the city. The family initiated the whaling industry and developed shipbuilding and sent ships to China and revived the city's business after the French revolution.

Thomas Dobree (1810-1895) the heir, had an incredible fortune in inheritance and fair play to the old mucker, he quickly stopped the family tradition of making money and devoted fifty years of his life and shed loads of cashola to collecting all kinds of works of art. Over this period Thomas collected some 10,000 works, including numerous masterpieces.

There is tonnes of stuff to gawp at. On the ground floor, the old beams and gargoyles and mainly, I suppose, churchy artefacts and weaponry, this is a must for any bloke who at one time in his life (from the age of three and up) wanted to go to war and butcher as many baddies as possible and become a hero for his hobby.

Armoury, sabres and guns and knives, wahey! Oh and if you wanted to be a man of the cloth, I'm sure you would find the more boring stuff of particular interest.

The first floor is home to mainly paintings, jewellery and such.

The paramount attraction of the museum though is the heart of Anne of Brittany. The heroine of the town has her heart (what's left of it anyway) encapsulated in a large golden heart shaped locket and suspended on wire in a glass casing. This is something definitely worth having a butchers at because of the importance of the woman in question. I stand and stare at the heart for a while, and wait 'till no one is around and ask the heart for a little help tonight against the Monegasques. Asking for a win from a rotten heart cannot be as bad as going to a church and praying to God, can it? I thought that there was no harm done anyway. Just maybe the spirit of the former Queen of France and Duchess of Brittany could stop this losing streak and bring us some needed, not to mention warranted points.

The stadium seems as packed as it was previously for the P.S.G. game, just not as fierce.

I look down at the Brigade and I wish I were with them but if anything happened to my arm I think Madman's patience would wear thin with my exploits of recent times, so a decent view of the game will have to suffice.

The F.C.N.A. line up without Da Rocha, which is a bit of a worry, but it seems that Deschamps has left Giuly on the bench, which of course is a good sign.

In the first half there was much slipping all over the shop from the outfield players as the rain kept on coming and the pitch was getting greasier by the minute making it very hard to control the ball to mount any kind of attack from either side. Most of the action takes place in midfield.

The first real attack from Nantes comes from the creative stimulus that is Ziani. The little man links with Sauvinaud who puts the ball through to Pujol, Pujol shoots but Flavio Roma saves well, he has quickly become accustomed to the conditions that the Atlantic coast weather has served up for tonight's encounter. The weather makes me think to myself about an extremely stupid French saying I seem to hear quite often on my travels to this city. Every time it rains, someone always says to me 'English weather', which is followed by a sly little grin from the culprit and a giggle. Now, I'm not one for Frog bashing, but have a word with yourselves Northern French, almost every time I've been here, bar my summer road trip, the weather has hardly been exotic to say the least.

The young canaries' forward, Ahamada, hits a long ranger from twenty-five yards out and it narrowly goes wide of Roma's post. Christ's teeth, the boys in yellow are playing well, most of the possession, but no cigar. Something's gotta' give. Come on Anne, sort me out here. I can't go home again without seeing a goal from the boys of the Beaujoire.

Armand gathers the ball on the left, passes to Toulalan, who, oh my God, he's through on goal, it's an open goal, put it in the fucking goal please…Shower of cunts, a Monaco defender appears from nowhere and clears the fucker off the line. Bollocks!

Halftime. This is painful.

The second half begins with the same energy as the end of the first. Nantes look great and their passing is sublime but then again it has been for most of the season so far to be honest, the problem is the lack of shots on goal.

More chances and my previous argument is out of the window, Roma is just too damn good, or he has been blessed. Maybe by Anne of Brittany, maybe she was disappointed by an English Nantes fan praying to her for a win and is punishing me for the blasphemy I earlier initiated.

At the other end Morientes gets a decent enough chance but puts it wide, luckily.

Deschamps brings on Giuly and suddenly the Monegasques seem to step up a gear, they have not come here for the draw, although at the moment, even with Nantes playing the better football, I'd settle for a draw.

Not to be, I'm afraid. Bernardi in the 77th minute beats Landreau. 1-0. Unreal. No matter how well we are going to play I know already we're not going to get anything back. The God's are against us… Again.

My trudge back through the crowds away from Beaujoire and towards the tram is pleasant enough given the circumstances. The last three trips out to Nantes have not given me the greatest amount of oomph to write enthusiastically about football. Three home games, three 1-0 defeats.

The trams are totally rammed so I decide to walk back into town, which takes about an hour and I recommend it because the areas you pass by are not the places that you would see if you came to visit the city and so they are sadly overlooked. Not exactly suburbia, but close. It's Saturday night and the place is so quiet, light relief from the hustle and bustle in the ground.

I make it to Georgia and David's new apartment and although the furniture is still sparse it seems to make little difference to the fifteen odd people lazing around the floor warming up for a party. I see a few faces I recognise and a few that I don't. I say my greetings to the ones I know and then also to the ones I don't.

There goes the idea of an early night in preparation for the people from the council, but what can I do? What would you do? I know what I'd do, and that's what I did, and that's why I can't remember anything to tell you about, except that we went to another party about two in the morning. At this party I met a guy who supported St. Etienne. He told me Nantes were shit and I told him he may have a point at the moment but that I was confident we could bounce back, and what the fuck did he know anyway, his team were still in the second division?

The Sunday went as smooth as I could have hoped for. Our guests for the evening both seemed to like me but there really was not much they could do to help, apart from tell the club about my idea and try to get a meeting with them.

This, I must admit, pissed me off a little. Looking back I was selfish and stupid to think that these lovely people would simply champion my idea and take it to the council to publish. Firstly it is written in English, secondly they have no idea if I can write or not, and maybe after all this I can't.

Shit! Fuck! Shitfuck!!

8

"They're bound to lose with a name like that"
Dave, Barman, John McByrne pub, 2003

Toulouse, home of fantastic sausages. Apart from meaty stuff, it also plays host to a very well renowned rugby team, the current European Champions, no less.

One thing it is not is a footy town.

This is why Toulouse find themselves pasted to the bottom of the league with Le Mans for comfort. Nantes are in eighth place, as we lost away to Lille: 2-0. But still, we might as well be top of the league for all Toulouse care, as they have only won two of their sixteen matches in the league so far this season.

I had noticed that our goal difference went down an awful lot recently due to so many defeats, we are now on zero, but even this looks fancy when compared to Toulouse's minus sixteen.

Sitting on the plane reading these facts I can't help but laugh. Maybe it's because Toulouse look so weak, Nantes can really make up for their lack of goals in this one and stick a few past the hapless Revault and his pathetic defence.

Or maybe I'm laughing more out of the knowledge that this is the first time in a long time that I haven't feared the opposition and actually believe, whole heartedly, that we will win tonight.

Although Nantes' league form hasn't been amazing recently, they have progressed to the next round of the Coupe de la Ligue, beating Nancy 3-1 after extra time. A good cup run is exactly what they, and the supporters need.

Tonight's line up is likely to be Landreau in goal, Savinaud, Delhommeau, Gillet and Armand in defence. Pujol is out, so I expect to see N'zigou up front and the return of Da Rocha in midfield.

After the Lille game they must have been well low. The way they played against Monaco was superb and they were so unlucky not to get a result. Away to Lille is never going to be easy. I've been told the stadium is quite foreboding and normally sold out as Lille is very much a football town; kind of like Lens, but even so, when is this losing streak going to come to some sort of climax?

40 years in Ligue 1, it might not be 41 at this rate. Amisse needs to give the players a proper kick up the arse.

What they need is a bit of the old Vince Lombardi treatment. I am currently reading one of the all-time-classic American sport books, 'Instant Replay'.

It's written over the course of one season in the NFL by line backer Jerry Kramer while with the Green Bay Packers. It is a phenomenal book and Lombardi; the half-saint-half-monster coach comes across as a very frightening, but talented, individual who inspires those around him. He seems like the kind of boss you need to succeed, but you'd rather be a loser than have him around.

I wander to a cyber net café to look at the latest goings on at the club. Tonight there will be twenty minutes silence, the first twenty minutes of the game. This will not only be at Beaujoire but at every ground in the country. It is organised by the Ultras and obviously the Brigade Loire are running da shit down at the Beaujoire.

The silence is a protest against the clubs because the fans are pretty much fucked off with the way they are being treated. The taking away of the terraces, the higher rates they have to pay to watch football (don't move to England whatever you do, you'll go postal). The banning from the grounds of flares and confetti??

How can you ban confetti? 'Excuse me sir this confetti is dangerous, put it out or I will have to report you'.

Lazy buggers, they just don't want to clear it up.

So I presume the silence is to show the club that the whole spectacle is pretty boring without the fans making noise and cheering on the team, it is to show the clubs that they need their fans and should treat them with a little bit more respect.

If Toulouse score early on though, I can't imagine that the Brigade will be able to suppress their anger and the silence may be broken.

Before all of this though, I wander over to the cathedral, St. Pierre. The nicest way to stroll to the cathedral is via the Chateaux, up Cours

St. Pierre, which is an 18th century dirt and gravel boulevard, massively wide, and its space makes a great impression on your left hand side; this is the dark walled side of the castle and the cathedral, compared to its lighter counterpart on your right, which is lined with grandiose houses (now probably apartments), one of which, I am told was the home of one Thomas Dobree, and is now a hotel. At the very end of the boulevard is Place Marechal Foch, where an enormous column with a monument of Louis XVI stands.

The Cathedral is massive and partly derelict on the outside. On my visit, half of the front façade is covered in scaffolding, due to a spruce up; once finished it will probably be as gleaming clean and white as its slightly smaller companion church, St. Croix, tucked away in Bouffay.

In 1972 there was a fire at the cathedral which destroyed a good part of its interior and this is more than likely the reason it feels so sanitised and pristine now.

The main interest of the interior is the tomb of Francois II, the duke of Brittany and his two wives. The Duke and his second wife, who was the mother of Anne of Brittany. The corner statues show portrayals of Justice, Fortitude, Temperance and Prudence. The statue representing Justice is believed to be a portrait of Anne of Brittany.

Anne commissioned this tomb and before she died she asked for her heart to be placed in it. Her wish was granted but Thomas Dobree must have been a pretty good grave robber...

After a coffee to contemplate and digest my latest findings, I wander back into Bouffay, the heart of the city.

There isn't as much literature available about St. Croix but all I can do is recommend it as highly as its larger friend. The Loire limestone is so bright that the front façade actually looks like some kind of over the top Christmas cake, complete with a golden choir of angels plonked on top of it.

The choir of angels is actually part of the belfry and reminds me of the out of tune chimes of the Swiss Centre in Leicester Square.

Inside St. Croix I take a pew and let my eyes do the walking, a few hardliners are praying to their Catholic God, either for forgiveness or just through Catholic guilt. It's all a little amusing and bewildering, especially when you hear the tinkle of Euros falling into the collection boxes as people enter and leave, yet the homeless person begging outside gets fuck all, apart from some first class acting via his tunnel-vision adversaries who pretend to ignore him whilst he blocks most of the doorway. Now that's what I call turning the other cheek.

As St.Croix is literally around the corner from the John McByrne, I decide that it would be terribly rude of me not to go inside and see those friendly faces.

Dave believes Nantes will win tonight, I take his view on board, then realise I am listening to the opinion of a Brummie P.S.G. fan. 'Come on, they're bound to lose with a name like that!'

Groans from around the bar and Dave acknowledges that his joke was indeed bollocks.

It makes a nice change to get on the tram to Beaujoire and not be pissed. But the ride is a lot more boring because of it. Not having the nagging sensation of needing to pee is a relief, but the journey does seem twice the length than usual.

The lads are warming up when I get to the ground. Tonight, I think I will look for my allocated seat as the place looks like it isn't going to fill up for the visit of the mighty Toulouse. It takes me a while, but I find my own little plastic coated concrete step with my number, 212, in row ZH. Only problem is that it is obvious that nobody cares that it is my seat and I should go and find one that is empty. Fuckers, I really wanted to sit in my own seat, just for one game.

I realise that when reading this it sounds quite possessive and that there is nothing uglier that someone who is ruled by their possessions… But, and noted it is a very small, quite meaningless but, but a but all the same, I find it very strange owning something, yet never being able to use it, or touch it or do frankly any fucking thing with it. Yes sir, I'm not digging that weirdo vibe.

If I had big enough balls and a decent bite of the French lingo, I would have made sure that that sucker moved, then I would have taken a shit on my seat, because after that, my friends, nobody will go near my seat.

It would be mine forever, even when my season ticket is eventually passed on to the new cardholder and seat owner, no-one will sit in my coveted seat, because, he/she will know, just like all those others who witnessed the event at the Toulouse match back in 2004 that this seat belongs to 'Crazy shit man.'

Where was I? Oh yes, Toulouse, Toulouse, they're going to fucking Toulouse!

By the time of kick off there must have been under thirty thousand spectators in the ground, which I believe is probably the lowest I have seen all season.

Basically the Loire end was over half empty, with Brigade pretty much turning their backs on the team. I had moved down to the front to see if I could see X, but I couldn't, so I took a seat on the front row of the right hand side.

I must have had twenty to thirty seats to myself. And the overwhelming quietness of the stadium during those twenty minutes was very surreal. I didn't really know what to do with myself, so I did what I normally do when I don't know what to do, smoke.

Looking at the team my presumed line up was wrong. Da Rocha was playing up front with Vahirua and N'Zigou was on the bench. Why on earth was Amisse playing a winger up front, and not a very tall one either if he was going to act as a target man for the dwarf-like Vahirua?

Glombard was playing in Da-Rocha's usual position of right wing, apart from that everything was pretty much normal, with the exception of Yepes, who was out with a suspension.

The game played in this strange and quiet atmosphere took on the exact same mood. It was dull, without the crowd it was nothing. The fans were right, no doubt about it. It could have been the great Ajax side of the seventies, the Milan of Sacchi or even an all star game with Pele, El Diego, Cruyf and Lee Dixon, but it wouldn't matter, even with the flashes of brilliance it would still be like watching Sunday league. I am a lover of grass roots footy, but given a chance between a professional game and an amateur, I will always go for the pro.

So there you go, when your kids look up to you while watching the Brockley Bulldozers, or whatever on a Sunday morning and ask you what the difference is between professional football and the crap they are watching just tell them, professional football is louder.

As soon as the twenty minutes were up, on the second, no word of a lie, the game changed. In the twentieth minute the flags went up and the shouting started. Armand the left back smacked the ball from outside the box and the shot was saved instinctively by Revault. Vahirua runs into the box and is caught, he goes down. It's a penalty.

Gillet, one of my favourite players places the ball. Oh yes, this could be the start of rout and the end of the famine.

Whack!!!!!!!!!!

It's the first Nantes goal I have seen in ages, and I dance around my empty part of the stadium, all by myself.

Da Rocha seems to be taking to the role of forward rather well under the circumstances, but Nantes cannot breakdown Toulouse enough to be able to get sufficient strikes on goal. Toulalan has a chance but it is well saved.

Half time comes and a pretty dry game comes to a halt.

The second half starts as blandly as the first finished. Balmont has a shot and Glombard touches the ball with his hand in the area, shit.

This time Toulouse have a penalty and Dieuze, the lone Toulouse forward, places it past Landreau. 1-1.

And that is how it finished, as dull as dishwater and just as tasty. Two penalties is all the game deserved. Because of this piss poor result Nantes drop two places to tenth and it looks like they can kiss the champions league spot a not so fond farewell. Even the Uefa cup now looks a long way away, unless they have a good cup run.

I begin to wonder if I have made a mistake…

9

Corsicans & Car Bombs

The next couple of weeks are very frustrating. The next away game is against fellow Bretons; Guingamp, it ends in a 1-1 draw. The next home game is against Auxerre, and I cannot get a flight as they are sold out. The Auxerre game ended in a 1-0 victory. No, you're eyes are fine.

That was the last game before the traditional Christmas break, the next home game is not until the 17th January.

The first game after the Christmas break is against Lens, away. This ends in a 0-0 draw, which is not too bad a result to be honest, as Lens is a tough place to go to get anything.

And so, here I am, on another bloody plane, having spent another bloody £120 to bloody get it. It's 2004, people, and we are rocking. Maybe we're not too hot in the race for the championship (currently 10th), but we are kicking serious arse in the Coupe De La Ligue.

On the 17th December we beat Clermont Foot to go through to the quarterfinal.

The game was played at Beaujoire and finished 0-0 after 90 minutes. One minute before penalties Yepes scored (119th min) to put le Canaris through.

The quarterfinal was away to neighbours Le Mans on January 14th. Moldovan marked his return with a goal in the 63rd minute, only for it to be cancelled out three minutes later when Hautcoeur scored for Le Mans. So the game went to extra time and then to penalties. It finished 5-4 to Nantes, and we are in the semi final, which is to be played on either 3rd or 4th of February. My God, imagine. A trip to the Stade de France could be on the cards. Suddenly the last few games have been forgotten and we are now in a great position to qualify for Europe.

In the Coupe de France we played Beaujolais on the 4th of January and won 2-1.

Tonight we entertain the Corsicans, Ajaccio. As my small, tin-can-excuse of a plane lands at Nantes Atlantique, I see a plane with the company logo of Corsair splashed across it, the Corsicans have landed. They have arrived for their annual hiding.

Oh yes, I am in confident mood. A couple of weeks away from my spiritual home has replenished my appetite. I'm back, so stand back chicken scraps, 'cause I ate more turkey than Bernard Matthews and I'm ready to blow (off, not job).

The airport is as bustling as it always is on a Saturday morning; the only difference is that there are armed police around. Whether this is France's answer to 'the war on terror' or just because they are worried about Corsican separatists I couldn't tell you, but it was certainly a little bit more on the tense side than usual.

I get the bus to Commerce, as usual, and on the trip leaf through a L'Equipe that I picked up for free from the plane.

Tonight, now that January's transfer window has opened, Moldovan can start and I am relishing his return to the Beaujoire for a league game. He will probably line up in attack with Vahirua.

When I get to Commerce, I make my way to Planete F.C.N.A. (the Nantes FC shop). I try to explain to the bewildered man behind the counter that I would like an away ticket for the match in Bordeaux. He explains that you cannot buy them in Nantes, and have to get them at the stadium in Bordeaux on the day.

Last week when, unusually, I had some extra cash I decided to book online and get a flight to Bordeaux, it would be my first away game. The shop attendant then tells me that the game may well be televised and that I shouldn't book my flight just yet, as the fixture could be moved to a different evening to accommodate the television channel that has purchased the rights to it.

Great!

This could mean that I have spent another hundred quid, for no reason. A little pissed off, I stroll down to Passage Pommeraye to pick up the keys from the jewellery shop. The owner passes the keys to me. It appears that David and Georgia are not in Nantes, this weekend which means I have the flat all to myself.

The flat is very tidy and I desperately need some kip, so I flake out for a couple of hours.

After a shit, shower and shave, I go in search of more of the wonders that this compact little city has to offer. I decide to go on one of the walks that are recommended in my Brittany guidebook. The author Phillipe Barbour's book for Cadogan Guides is exhaustive in its detail of Brittany, and if you are going to stay in Nantes I recommend the purchase of it as its guide to the city is very straightforward and just about everything worth seeing is inscribed within.

I walk to Rue d'Orleans, which leads to Place Royal. The square was designed by the architect Crucy. In the centre there is a grand fountain made from what looks like granite. The figure in the centre holding a trident symbolises the city of Nantes, and the trident and its holder crop up regularly around the city, and at the stadium too, adorning flags and the like. Around the figure the Loire and its tributaries shed water back into the basin.

To the northeast of Place Royal are Place Fournier and the Basilique St-Nicolas. The Basilique is a neo-gothic church, which I first mistook for the cathedral St. Pierre. It is easy to do as St. Nicolas is enormous. Again, like St. Pierre, it has a lot of scaffolding around it due to the cleaning process that is taking place, but the spire is now finished and it reaches 85 metres; you can see its spire in any part of central Nantes. Keep walking north and you come to Nantes' obligatory eye sore. The Tour de Breatgne is a sorry excuse for a skyscraper. It is a brown block, around half the size of Canary Wharf and looks out-dated and out of place. Although Nantes, like any other city, has some ugly buildings such as Molokoff (an estate on the outskirts), most of the city is very pleasing on the eye, and then you turn around another delicately detailed corner and boom! The giant browner stares you right in the face. I am sure the views from the Tour de Bretagne are quite spectacular and I am sure at one point I will go up and take a peak, it is just a pity it looks like it does from the outside.

Still, if you go south of Place Royal rather than north, you can quickly get over the misery of the brown tower. Place de Commerce is the bustling square that the airport arrives in and is probably the central nervous system of the city. If you stand with your back to Place Royal you'll see, directly in front of you, the tram line that runs to the Chateaux, the train station and eventually to Beaujoire and the stadium. To your right is the multi media shop Fnac that was another Crucy design; an architect who was heavily influenced by the total genius of Ettienne Louis Boullee. If you do not know Boullee's work then I recommend Peter Greenaway's beautiful film, 'The Belly of an Architect', in which most of his designs are shown.

The Crucy building is called The Bourse and was completed in 1812 as a business exchange building, hence why the square is called commerce. It is one of Nantes' finest lumps of cement and stone with its huge Romanesque pillars at the entrance.

To your left is a row of shops and cafes, which are totally rammed as soon as a bit of sun comes out. One of which, the Café de Commerce, is wonderful with its colonial-feel interior.

If you walk to the centre of the square, behind to your right is the modern cinema multiplex owned by Gaumont. Only a company as powerful as Gaumont could have a design so ridiculously misplaced and dumped in the middle of such a square. It isn't that the modern building is particularly ugly, it just so doesn't belong there!

Commerce can also be a little annoying. It is teeming with young students, all shouting over each other in idle conversation; which is not the annoying part (I, too, was a student with a rather large voice). The annoying part is it seems that it has become the fashion to ask for money when you are dressed from head to toe in middle class clothing. This is an outrage, I have been asked for money more times than I can remember every time I have walked through commerce, and not one of the people who has asked for cash is homeless. This is hard to prove, and I know what I said when I was in Lyon, but this is a piss take.

I would love to see some of the Barbour wearing gits outside the Gare Parreche in Lyon dare to ask for money while the true homeless watch on. They would be crucified. The cheeky gits, not the homeless, you understand.

Commerce is also a meeting point for demos and so on, and you can regularly see desks set up for petitions against right wing goings on.

Back to Place Royal, and onto the street Rue Crebillon that links Place Royal to its cousin Place Graslin (pronounced grarlan). This is another Crucy design and is host to the opera house, Theatre de Graslin; along with The Bourse and St. Croix it is one of my favourite buildings in Nantes. The first performance held here was in 1788; I think it was Rod Stewart. This is also where the F.C.N.A anthem 'the heart of the stadium' was recorded by the resident Opera Company.

Opposite the theatre is Nantes' favourite restaurant, La Cigale. I ate a meal here on a previous visit. The interior is fantastic, it is an art nouveaux fans dream, and it could well pass for Charles Rennie Mackintosh's French holiday home.

After my leisurely stroll, I head for the Bouffay quarter. Place de Bouffay used to be where the public executions took place but now has a flea market instead, which I guess is a little easier for the liberals to swallow.

I phone Xavier as I haven't seen him in ages. He is pleased to hear from me and we decide to meet after the game in the John McByrne. As soon as I put the phone down I know it is going to be heavy one. While I am here it would be rude of me not to pop into the afore mentioned public house to sample their exquisite, if rather expensive delights.

Dave is working and I give him a present I brought over for him. A Happy Mondays album he wants. He seems chuffed, which is good as it means that the first pint will be free. Dave tells me that after the visit of P.S.G. the Ultras of Nantes have jumped two places in the hooligan respect charts. (I'd like to hear Tony Blackburn count that one down. 'And now, in at number two. It's P.S.G. with their smash hit, "You're going home in Le' Ambulance").

He was informed of this by one of the Brigade Loire a few evenings ago. He doesn't know whether it is true and neither do I, but there has been talk that P.S.G. got the lumping they so deserved after the match. I ask Dave to put on Sky Sports so I can see the English scores. Wolves have beaten Man Utd. 1-0! I can't believe it and order another pint in celebration at this wonderful news. If Arsenal get a win tomorrow against Villa we will go top by two points.

Dave tells me of his New Year jaunt back to blighty and the gig he went to over the holiday period. He went to see current club favourite Mr. Scruff do a set in the capital. I went home to Norfolk and had sex with members of my family in the Fens (joke).

I pop over to the newsagent to pick up 'Jaunes de Coeur', F.C.N.A's monthly magazine.

Back in the boozer I leaf through it. It is an A4 size glossy with match reports, interviews, and of course, adverts. But not as many as you would expect. I am especially pleased I picked it up because the centrefold poster is the squad picture, albeit without the Romanian God, Moldovan.

Hetty will love this on the living room wall opposite my giant Ali poster, oh yes. This month there is an interview with the lanky striker Pujol. Pujol hails from Paris. Most people in the squad are from the Pays de Loire area, but there are a few that hail from elsewhere. Gillet is also from Paris, Da Rocha is from Bordeaux, in fact his brother, I believe, plays or used to play for Girondins. Fae is from the region along with Armand, Landreau, Berson, Toulalan, Delhommeau and Ziani.

Ajaccio should lose and, in my humble opinion, they could also be relegated come the end of the season. They have let in 26 goals so far, which is only six less than Guingamp who are third from bottom. Ajjacio are only four points off the bottom three also, so it doesn't look good.

But then again we should have done Toulouse, it didn't happen. Football is indeed a funny old game.

Just less than thirty thousand have turned up at the Beaujoire for the Corsicans and the tribune Loire is in full voice as the anthem blares around the stade. It is bloody freezing by the time the teams come out of the tunnel. And there he is in front of me for the first time, Viorel Moldovan.

The tannoy blares out the first names of the players as usual with their squad numbers and the stadium screams back their surnames with aplomb. When it comes to the Romanian he turns and salutes his adoring fans. 'Numero Neuf…Viorel' 'MOLDOVAN', huge applause to the number nine and chants of 'Viorel, Viorel' thunder around the ground. He has come to save our season from mediocrity!

The full line up is Landreau in goal, Gillet, Yepes and Guillon on defence. In midfield Da Rocha is back on the wing after his jaunt up front against Toulouse, then Fae and Berson in central midfield with Armand pushing up from left back to wingback. Ziani sits behind the front two of Vahirua and Moldovan.

We kick off and the confidence that has returned to the side with the return of Viorel is obvious. After only ten minutes we go one up. The ball comes to Vahirua and he whacks it, from inside the area.

Four minutes later Berson makes it 2-0. The first half goes by in a flurry. This is the best I have seen them play for a long time and actually reap the rewards they deserved in those 1-0 defeats I witnessed against the likes of Lyon and Monaco.

The only down side is Gillet getting booked for a lunge on Diomede. Half time and much hot coffee is required so I order four. Too much of this stuff could give you a heart attack, but at least I would die in the knowledge that we were winning for the first time in ages. Plus if I did die now, I wouldn't have to witness the throwing away of a 2-0 lead which is probably going to happen in the second half.

Some kids come onto the pitch for a half time major league soccer style penalty shoot out. They start in the centre circle and run at the approaching goalkeeper and try to put the ball past him, it has to be said that most of them do it with stunning accuracy. They must be aged from nine to twelve and all of them would be able to whip me. I don't mean that I would want them to literally whip me; I thought I better put that in, in case I am investigated.

The second half starts and Nantes are still in control; maybe they are not going to throw this one away.

Nine minutes in and Gillet collects the ball on the right and controls like a winger instead of the staunch centre back that he is, and passes the ball into the box. Moldovan collects and as Trevisan the Ajjacio keeper comes out he slashes it into the net.

Hysteria in the stadium. Moldovan makes it 3-0. He is most definitely back. His goals and penalties in the Coupe de La Ligue have been the warm up for his first league goal of the season.

The goal is announced and is responded to exactly as earlier. Moldovan runs to the Jules Verne stand, maybe where his family are sitting, looks up and the relief to be back is obvious. Vahirua jumps on his back and the start of a carnival gets underway.

Twenty minutes later Moldovan is substituted and is given a standing ovation.

N'Zigou comes on for him and immediately gets into gear.

There is five minutes of added time and N'zigou scores in the 84th. This must be some kind of joke. 4 – 0.

I leave the ground and head for the tram in a state of mild shock. A smile fixed on my face, one of those wonderful feelings of contentment after seeing your team win.

Not the kind of feeling you get when you watch a penalty shoot out and scrape through by the seat of your pants while you are touching cloth. Instead, that feeling when you see your team control a game from start to finish with total self belief that there will be only one outcome, and that is victory, my friends.

The tram is crammed to the hilt on the way back and I need to get out, so I get off a few stops early and walk from the Chateaux down Rue de Stalingrad to Bouffay. The John McByrne is teeming and I look around for Xavier, he's not here yet, but it is no surprise that he is late, he always is.

I sup a pint and have a chat with Joe, one of the barmen. A top bloke from the outskirts of London and it is nice to hear the accent of the south, as most English people I have met here seem to be from the miserylands, sorry, I mean the midlands.

The pub fills up very quickly after the game and I recognise a few faces from the Tribune Loire, some Brigade and some others.

Xavier eventually arrives and we quickly lay into the ale. Xav is doing up his house so he can rent it out and come over to England, he should be moving to London within a month as he has just left his job. He is naturally a little anxious, he is after all still a young man, and he is uprooting away from his native land.

We chat a bit about family gossip and drink and drink. Before we know it the lights go up and the game's over. It is slinging out time.

Dave and Joe ask us if we want to go for a late drink with them. 'Late? It's fucking half past two!'

Calloways is a bar which doesn't seem to close and we head off there and agree to meet Joe and Dave a little later as they have to clean up ashtrays, spilt beer and vomit in the bar.

By the time they meet us we are half cut, well, Xav is anyway; I'm totally cut. After a few arguments about politics and football I fall asleep at the bar.

About half past five Xavier wakes me and decides he'll take me home to Georgia's apartment as I have an early flight. He carries me out the door, I tell him it's okay he can let go of me as I am able to stand, he lets go and I fall over. Much to the amusement of the Calloway. Gits.

It is very late and the city is deserted, once I can actually walk we stumble through Graslin and up Rue Racine. We stop at a corner where no one can see us, and I start to throw up and Xavier takes a piss. I find the whole thing extremely funny and laugh through chokes of vomit. I'm sure my Mother wouldn't find it funny. Just as we both finish depositing our bodily fluid and gunk, the most almighty crash I have ever heard explodes in my ears.

The walls shake! Xavier ducks for cover: I kneel in my own sick. 'Shit!'

'What the fuck was that?' I ask.

'Fuck knows' replies Xavier 'but it was loud'.

Loud it was indeedio, my friend. My ears are still ringing.

We get to the apartment and try the keys in the door but for some reason it won't open. Xavier tries it again, still no joy. I take a seat on the stairs and watch in amusement.

It won't budge, so we try to throw ourselves at it to break it down. This is ridiculous. Two men jumping at a door, at dawn, waking up the neighbours. Just the thought of trying to break down the door of our joint sister-in-law is totally out of order, I don't know what we would have done if we had actually succeeded and I'm surprised the police never showed up.

Eventually the door opens, and some bloke is standing in the doorway. Our first thought is that we have been trying to break into the wrong apartment. But it turns out that the geezer is a friend of David's and is staying the night.

We apologise, but really want to smack him one as we had been at the door for about forty minutes.

We get inside and disgustingly open some beer. I take one sip and decide enough is enough. We put on the local T.V channel to see if there is any report on the explosion we heard.

Xav takes my phone and sets the alarm, and that was that.

I wake up at midday in last night's clothes with the hangover of the year so far, as it is only January I'm sure there will be worse to come. I look at the clock on my phone and brick it. I have missed the plane. I can't believe it.

I panic, but there is fuck all I can do about it. Maybe I can exchange it at the airport but it's unlikely, but under the circumstances it's worth a shot.

I get in a cab to the airport and try to explain my situation to the Air France desk; they are having none of it.

Usually I wouldn't panic too much, but I've got three meetings tomorrow and my numbers from quotes have been bad so far in 2004 and I need to impress the boss a bit. It is safe to say that being stuck in France due to sleeping through my alarm clock thanks to stupid amounts of alcohol intake is not going to impress him. Some people are just weird.

I phone Xavier and explain what has happened. I am going to have to stay at his place tonight and phone some people for some money as I spent my wages the previous evening. Xavier agrees to pick me up in a couple of hours, as he has nobody to watch the kids.

I find my phone card and try Het, she doesn't answer. I phone Mat and tell him, he doesn't have any money, but he will keep trying Het for me. I am about to phone Madman and tell him my troubles, then I remember that my Grandmother has recently sold her flat and given the money to her kids, i.e. my Dad is rolling in the lolly at the moment.

I phone him and of course he has a major go at me for not being able to grow up e.t.c. I shout back and ask him blatantly for £200, so I can at least get home on Monday morning.

He agrees to put the money in the bank first thing tomorrow, as today is Sunday.

I fall asleep feeling stupid and a little sorry for myself. Three hours later Xavier shows up and buys me a coffee. I am thankful, that he has come, although he is of course later than he said he would be.

He takes me to Air France desk and buys me a ticket on his credit card for a flight home later that day. I will be eternally thankful to Xavier. And my old trick of finding money from nowhere is again erupting like a volcano of joy.

Xav explains that the crash last night was a car bomb. It was the Ambassador's car outside his house. Nobody was hurt. Nobody knows who it was.

Nice.

On the plane I thank my lucky stars and gulp the complimentary coffee. And I think to myself of how to spend the £200 that my Dad is about to put into my bank account. This is going to be a good week! Wahey!

10

Away Day

The following week is as chaotic as the previous. The Bordeaux game is moved from the Saturday evening to the Friday as to accommodate the T.V audience. Thus my flight ticket is now completely useless.

With Dad's kindly loaned £200 I go to my travel agent and try to buy a ticket for the upcoming Nice game but both flights to Nantes have sold out. Whether this is because Nantes has become a bastion for the romantically inclined as it is Valentine's Day, I don't know. One thing is for sure I am pissed off that I won't be in France, but her indoors is happy.

While all these balls-ups were happening, a semi-final took place for the Coupe de La Ligue. Nantes took on Auxerre at Beaujoire on Tuesday the 3rd of Feb. It ended 0-0. I was in The Wickham Arms, watching the semi-final of the English equivalent between my beloved Arsenal and Middlesborough with my Godson, Toby, who had just moved down to London.

To make sure I was kept up to date, Laurie kept phoning me as he was on the web for most of the evening researching something, which I forget now.

The French game went to penalties, and in the middle of the pub, during the weekly pub quiz, Laurie reported the live transmission.

Landreau's hero status jumped through the roof as he saved penalties, two of which had to be retaken, probably due to him moving off his line, and then, to win the game and put us through to the final, he stepped up for the final penalty and scored!

Fucking magic, I was extremely happy and screamed in the silence of the quiz night and was duly asked to leave. Yeah well, that pub stinks anyhow.

We are going to Paris! The Stade de France awaits, and somehow I have to get a ticket.

But, more importantly, there is a big away game around the corner in one of the most interesting cities in Europe, Marseille.

Again short of the lolly, Madman stumps up the credit card, so at least I don't have to pay him until the end of the month. 'Two tickets please'. It is Hetty's birthday and so I'm sure she couldn't think of anything better than travelling to the south of France for a long weekend to watch a spot of the old footy.

Unbelievably she was overjoyed at the prospect and the tickets were duly purchased.

We call Georgia to see if they know anybody in Marseille that maybe can put us up. She does, Peggy and Eric and their daughter Olive all live in central Marseille and would love to have us. Resulto!

Hetty has already met Peggy and Eric, so a little familiarity will help the situation.

On the Friday, the day of travel, I get ready to leave work early so I can get to the airport when Georgia phones. It turns out that Peggy has phoned her in Nantes to tell her that the airport may be closed because the city is on 'Alert Orange'. Marseille suffers from very heavy winds especially this time of year. One wind in particular the Mistral is a chilly, powerful bugger and not to be sniffed at. I remember the last time we were there, last summer and I was talking to a guy who was sleeping rough and he said even he had to move away from Marseille in the winter because of the Mistral, because it was so hard to sleep through.

I phone Gatwick and the British Airways desk and they inform me that they haven't heard a thing, which, hey, is totally reassuring.

On the flight after take off the pilot informs us that we will experience some very high winds as we approach Marseille, 'It will get a little bumpy'.

YOU RECKON?

Christ on a bike. Undoubtedly the most terrifying landing I have known, although I pretended I wasn't bothered at all as Hetty's hand was strapped to my thigh giving me the worst horse bite known to man.

In fact the pain in my leg took away the stress of the landing, so I guess I should thank her for the rather large purple bump I now have.

Just as we came in to land over the harbour a gust of wind came from underneath the plane and must have hit the wing as it knocked us sideways. A girl in the row opposite us was in tears and people were beginning to get very nervous. Eventually, we landed safely but it was a bit of a nail biter and an anal loosener.

We took the shuttle bus in to central Marseille and then a cab to Peggy's apartment where she was waiting with beer and Pastis. For someone who informed Georgia that she doesn't speak any English she does a very good job and makes the situation a lot easier for us ignoramuses.

We hit the sack with the winds blasting against the windows and are woken when one of the communal windows in the hall is blown through. We go back to sleep, as there isn't anything that we can do about it anyway.

In the morning we meet the delightful Olive. Olive was born in Marseille four years ago, but her parents are Nantais and moved south seven years ago. Olive is excited by our company and cannot understand why we cannot speak to her fluently and thinks this is because we are special. Well of course we are, we're from the Empire my dear.

We all set off to try to find tickets to tomorrow's match and Marseille looks like Peckinpah's tobacco stained Mexico. The gale has brought the Sahara with it and the place is covered in sand.

We head to the Old Port and to the OM café (Olympic Marseille) where we can buy tickets. It is only then that Peggy realises that it is Nantes we are going to see and she wants to come too, and so does young Olive. I buy four tickets in the Tribune Ganay at thirty euros each for the adults and fifteen for Olive. Everyone is duly excited, I am a little disappointed that we won't be with the Nantes fans, but the ticket seller says that we cannot buy away tickets here, you have to buy them in Nantes. The guy in the Nantes shop said you have to buy away tickets from the club and city you are visiting and so it seems nobody really knows what they are talking about.

By the afternoon Marseille looks like Marrakech.

Peggy takes us on a tour of this amazing city and we head down the Corniche, which is the beach road, running from the Old Port down to the quaint village-like Malmousque. Walking around the small town within a town we are greeted by a Breton flag and I take this as a good omen for an away win tomorrow.

We take a bus to the centre called The Prado, this is where the Vellodrome, OM's daunting stadium can be found. The bus driver drove like he was running late for a hot date with the supermodel of his choice.

We get a bite to eat and sit in a café as the rain starts to come down. Hopefully, this will settle the dust and I won't have to spend the rest of the weekend squinting like Clint Eastwood.

Hetty and I start to put together a guest list for our forthcoming engagement party. One possibility that we haven't decided on is Hetty's cousin Jack. I am yet to meet young Jack, who has recently lost his father, poor soul and is renowned as a bit of a handful. Although he sounds like a total nightmare you cannot help but admire his archaic intelligence, which is ingenious, foul and very amusing. A couple of weeks ago, back in his hometown of Brighton, Jack wandered into a chip shop and somehow stole the vinegar bottle from the top of the counter. He went outside, found a quiet corner, emptied the vinegar from the bottle and duly filled it up with his own piss.

He returned the vinegar bottle to the counter, sat outside for the afternoon, gleefully watching the chip shop clientele douse the food in his piss and gulp it down.

Okay, not very nice, but as I said, ingenious and funny.

Peggy is much amused by the little horror's gamesmanship as are we all, but whether I want him at my engagement party, drinking what I think is champagne only for it to turn out to be his bladder oil; well, that's another kettle of fish.

Tonight we hit the town, Peggy gets a friend to baby-sit and she takes us to some of her locals.

Our first stop is Le Petit Nice. A large bar, usually packed, due to its less than expensive drinks list. It is hard to get in the door and even harder to get a table, but we manage both. The place is a real buzz. Waitresses somehow manage to remember where you are and bring drinks to you while dancing around obstacles.

Highly recommended indeed.

Behind the bar, with arms firmly crossed, is the owner, a former boxing champion. It is his presence, which keeps the calm, no doubt, as you wouldn't complain about the toilets, never mind the staff, to him. As good as any bar I have visited, but one you certainly wouldn't want to work in on a bad day.

We then head to the other side of Place Jean-Jaures to a Jazz bar called Pelle Melle. Tonight a reggae/ska band is playing and is bringing the house down even as we enter. 'Pressure drop' is blaring around the small intimate venue and we all undertake lots of drinking and a lot of dancing.

Upstairs there is a slightly calmer atmosphere if you need to wind down in a large lounge area. Peggy is looking forward to the return of Eric as he has been away acting for two weeks and she and Olive miss him dearly. Peggy is an actress also; it seems that everyone in France is either an actress or an artist.

By the time we return home we are too far gone and out, and the makeshift bed in the front room looks like pie and mash to a man starved of British grub.

In the morning I head out for some breakfast to Place Jean-Jaures and find numerous bakeries cooking fresh delights and return with fresh coffee and croissants.

Olive is in a more talkative mood as we have broken through the alien borders and are now friends. She is very excited about the game and will be supporting OM. Peggy will be rooting for her hometown and is looking forward to seeing Landreau play.

But before the game Peggy has to go and see a friend who has made chocolate cake and has invited friends over for the tasting.

The apartment is typical Marseille, huge windows and high ceilings. The cake is great, but time is getting on and I don't want to be late for the game. This must be seeping from my body as Peggy gets Olive ready and we head for the Stade Velodrome.

It is a short metro ride to the stadium and I am terribly excited about watching my team at an away game. Of course we will be in the Marseille end and I will not be able to shout for my team, but just to experience a different perception of supporting Nantes will be enough.

Inside, the ground is an awesome spectacle as the Ultras have probably been in their positions for a good hour or so. The kop ends in the ground are Virage Nord and Virage Sud. These are both covered in banners advertising the names of the fan camps. 'Commandos, Dodgers, Yankees and Ultras' are the main flags, plus two huge portraits, one of their prolific striker Drogba and one of Che.

The Virage Nord seems to be the slightly more hardcore of the two and they start the singing, chanting to the Virage Sud who duly reply. I don't think I have witnessed such a raucous crowd as this before. Even the infamous IRR of Lazio didn't get this excited, nor in Rio at the Maracanna was the atmosphere so visible. The passion of the Marsellais for their club is very special and unique. It serves as a focal point for the enormous boiling pot of different races that have made Marseilles their home, Tunisian, Moroccan, Algerian to name but a few. In an area of France where the support for the Front National is rife, the Velodrome is a haven where all are welcome, as long as you are for OM.

The Nantes team come out to warm up and are booed as expected. The small amount of Nantes fans that have made the trip try to break through the blanket of sound, but to minimal effect, although Landreau responds with a wave.

Nantes line up with Moldovan and Pujol up front, with the new number ten Yapi behind them, who seems to be a replacement for Ziani. Da Rocha on the right wing and Armand as the left wing back, with the ever-improving Emerson Fae and Nicolas Savinaud in central midfield. Gillet, Yepes and Delhommeau in defence. Up front for Marseille and a particular nuisance to defences everywhere this season is the prolific Drogba, he is partnered by Fulham reject Marlet.

In goal is the living legend of French football, Fabien Barthez. He was brought back from Manchester United to the French league after coming off the boil last season. Although he is much loved as both a player and a person in France, especially here in Marseille where he won the European cup, it seems a little unfair that he has displaced the perfectly capable Gavanon just so he can play regular football to stay in the international team.

The game starts in a mild manner and neither side seems to be looking for the win. The ball is played down the wings to little effect by both sides and the idea of passing through the middle of the park in the early stages looks like a no no.

There really isn't much to report until Armand fouls, what looks like Ferreira on the left. I can't really see how bad it was, but the stadium erupts in celebration as Armand is sent off.

'This could be the start of something terrible', I say to Hetty, and a lonely yellow and green figure about ten rows in front of us makes extremely rude gestures to the referee. I suppose you have to admire his bravery.

Marseille find their feet against ten men and Drogba scores his 14th league goal of the season and things are looking grim for the travelling Nantais.

But just before half time, the ball breaks for the inform Viorel Moldovan, he runs, and he shoots, and he fucking well scores a beauty. 1-1. The place goes silent, to our right we can see yellow and green and black/white Breton flags flapping around like crazy in this meanest of winds.

At half time the mood around the ground is not so good. The OM fans are very disappointed and nothing short of a second half onslaught will suffice. I am finding it all rather amusing.

More bemusing than amusing though is the design of this fine stadium. I believe it was once a cycling stadium, but even so. Only one very small amount of the ground is covered, of course this is the presidential area. If the winds in winter are terrible and rain is pretty much a cert, then why put a football team (football being a sport played in winter) into a fucking cycling stadium?

The architect must have been a total loon.

The second half produces chance upon chance for Marseilles, but our defending is very astute. Gillet, who has been booed every time he gets the ball, is playing fantastically along with Yepes as they soak up attack after attack. I wonder whether it is the fact that Gillet is Parisian that he is getting so much grief, as the derby of France between OM and P.S.G. is the most frenetic in the country.

Probably more to do with the fact he hand balled in the area and got away with it though. Mmm, yes, that's probably it. That'll do it every time.

Pujol is taken off and Vahirua comes on and very strangely within ten minutes he is taken off, whether this is because he is too small for the high balls being dropped over the Marseille back men, who knows? One thing is for sure is he isn't a happy bunny. He shakes his head as he walks off and grabs his coat from the trainer; he gets to the bench and kicks profusely, then jumps in the air smashing his fist into the roof. He can't get his coat on and throws it around. One of the Nantes players finds it all a bit selfish, I presume, and pushes him away. Vahirua carries on his violent vendetta against his archenemy, the subs bench. Oh dear me.

I can understand the frustration he must be feeling, but maybe he could have waited until he was in the tunnel. Poor bugger that must have been quite humiliating. You can only hope it was for the good of the team.

The frustrations of the crowd are obvious as the game draws to an end and must be an absolute joy for the Nantes players to experience. 1-1 in the end is a fair result as neither side played amazingly; in fact the only players who really shone were the Nantes defenders.

We leave the stade all happy, it was Peggy and Olive's first match and they enjoyed it very much. They thank us for taking them and we go to a local café for a drink and wait for the metro crowds to die off a little as it was all a bit much for Olive.

Olive was tucked in by her Mum once we got home and slept with her match ticket in her hand, Allez.

Eric returned a moment later and we sat down and had drinks. Eric was totally knackered, but in good humour and was clearly pleased to see Peggy and Olive. We felt that we shouldn't really be there, and felt we had gatecrashed a welcome home party, but he soon put us straight. The next morning we drove around Marseille with the wind still smacking against us. And we drove to what Marseilles call the end of the world. It is not really the end of the world, more like the end of Marseille. If you take Corniche to this area you get to see a couple of very important landmarks. The first is the island Chateau d'If; this is where Dumas' hero Edmund Dantes escapes in the book 'The Count of Monte Cristo'. Peggy and Eric inform us that many people believe the story to be true and come to take photos for historic reasons. This is a daft as tourists to London believing that Sherlock Holmes was a real geezer.

Dick heads.

The second is a giant poster of Zinedine Zidane's face, splashed across the side of a building back on the mainland, under the brooding glare of Zizou are the words 'made in Marseille'.

Eric worked for three months in London, and while he drove us around the city for the last time, he told us of how easy it was for him to get a job. All he had to do was walk into a French restaurant, making sure it was owned by an Englishman, and five minutes later he was given the job of chef. Although he admits that he cannot cook.

'I was French, so I must be a great at cooking. So fucking stooopid!'

He makes us crack up with his memories of home and his preposterous London accent. 'Alrite mate, yeah, ya, fack uff, you kant. Taxi, taxi you wann u taxi… Kant'.

As we walk towards the check-in desk, we hear them leaving the airport. 'Goodbye mate, fak uf, kant, alrighte mate, kant.'

Legend.

11

Stay in Bed

Some days are made for sleeping through and some are made for waking up to. February 28th 2004 was made for sleeping through, although I, in all my infinite wisdom, decided to get out of bed again on a Saturday morning whilst it was pissing down with rain and the wind was howling at my windows, begging to be let in from the watery morn.

I looked outside into the black dawn and felt a little miffed, not at the fact of getting up to watch Nantes again, but more because the weather was total bollocks and mother nature seemed to be rubbing my nose in the fact that I live in a country where you are just supposed to accept these treacherous mornings and live with it!

I'm rambling, this much I know, but as I go over the notes from the Nantes versus Strasbourg weekend, rambling is pretty much spot on, because I spent the whole weekend in a knackered daze.

Hetty mumbled something as I kissed her goodbye for another time. I almost fell down the stairs due to my eyes not feeling entirely ready to embrace the idea of opening.

Out in the gale at the bus stop, I'm instantly in luck as the bendy bus no.436 that takes you directly to Victoria for the Gatwick Express comes along. The reason I love this bus more than any other is the fact that it is free. It's obviously not supposed to be gratis, but the fact that the Mayor and London Transport expect you to pay at the bus stop for a ticket before you get on, and the fact that there are never any ticket inspectors on these bendy busses beggars belief. It totally shows how out of touch the local government is with the average Londoner. Who the fuck is going to pay a quid when they don't have to? Not me anyway. Sorry Ken.

At New Cross, some geezers who have just finished their night out get on. They look like they have had a right royal time to me. I feel sick just looking at them munch down their kebabs, as half of the gunk falls onto their shoes while they try to communicate through drunken drawls and Turkish meaty delights. 'You want chilli sauce with that?' I think I'll eat breakfast a little later thank you.

Victoria station is its usual pretty self just before dawn. People who can't seem to remember where they live always seem to hang around here. One guy in a suit is perched bizarrely in an alcove and he's sound asleep. He sits squashed into an area about four feet in diameter and about six feet in the air. I wonder how the hell he even managed to get up there, he must have been totally messy to think that the area he was frequenting would be his most comfortable option for a night under the stars. He wants to watch himself; someone might take those Patrick Cox's off his feet. His feet look bigger than mine, so he's safe for now.

The Gatwick Express does little to cheer me up. This is a train where you have to pay £22 return and the journey takes 30 minutes. £11 for 30 minutes? Not exactly a bargain. There is another train that goes to East Croydon, where you can change for Gatwick which in all takes 45 minutes and is generally free (no conductors), but it doesn't run at this time of day.

I'm sorry I sound so miserable, but I've never been good at this morning trip stuff and today is no different.

The family sharing my table consists of three young boys who all seem extremely excited about going away on holiday. Naturally I want to have them shot. I try to get some sleep and I'm about to drop off when some mutton dressed as lamb asks me for my ticket. I want to take her ticket machine and club her to death, but I pay her and try to get some sleep. Then some even muttonier bird asks me if I would like a coffee, I want to pour scolding hot coffee over her eyes, but I buy a coffee and spend the rest of the DELAYED (yep £22 return for a delayed fucking trip) journey mumbling to myself and scaring the children around me.

At Gatwick the ponce on the Air France desk where I check in tells me that the plane is delayed.

Wow, now there's a surprise! I mean today of all days when I'm feeling on top of the world.

So, what to do? I plump for the top quality dining experience of Garbunkles. Most of the branches throughout London seem to have been geographically situated to rip off the tourists, but at airports they are still cooking on gas and kicking up a storm for all and sundry. What a wonderful bargain it is to pay close to a tenner for a full English with a cup of coffee. 'Hey do you want a refill?' 'No, I want a refund'.

An hour or so later the plane is still not ready to board, it turns out that the plane has not even left France. I go to the help desk, where of course I don't get any help. I'm feeling a Falling Down kind of mood coming on.

A group had gathered around the 'help' desk, for some answers. I felt a little sorry for the some mother's do ave' 'em look-alike on duty as he tried, mostly unsuccessfully, to deflect the barrage of cutting abuse coming his way. I love it when people complain about a company to one of their employees, because it always reminds me of a thick prat who starts an argument.

'I'm not a racist, but I can't stand those darkies/Yids/Pakis/Chinks' (the choice is yours). 'It's not your fault fella, but this is totally out of order!'

'I've got a meeting to get to.'

'I've got a wedding to get to.'

'I've got a funeral to get to.'

'Big fucking deal, I'm going to a football match, now grow up and stop whinging. I don't know'.

My attention is quickly focused on a couple at the front of the desk. The bloke seems to be hanging back a bit, a little embarrassed by his wife's stress at the whole situation. I feel terrible writing about it, but I'm finding it all rather amusing. This woman is steaming. More than likely she is bang in the middle of the menopause, and so it shouldn't be a laughing matter, but it is.

A couple next to me in the queue are already laughing at them. The poor cow is steaming, she is ready to explode, and keeps jabbing her hubby in the ribs and pulling his arm towards the desk expectantly. I don't know what she wants him to do. She is in a right state and this could get ugly. Almost as ugly as her.

The poor bugger who works for Air France, walks us through customs to pick up the cases that were never loaded onto the plane that never arrived. I try to state my claim to go straight on and not wait around, as I haven't got any, only hand luggage. I'm informed that my request is impossible and I'll have to wait for everyone else.

The stress ball is almost foaming at the mouth as we walk to another help desk, she is a ball of rage lashing out at her bloke, and trying to keep the venom under her breath, but not succeeding. It sounds a little like this 'Well, really, I don't see why gggrrrrrhhghghgdhhhrr ggggggggrrrrrrrrrrrrrrrr!!!!!!!!!'

Air France has decided to put us on a British Airways Flight to Paris, where we can get a connection to Nantes.

A group of us are waiting to board, but there is a problem, two of the passengers are missing, we look around and we know automatically know who they are. A cloud of stress suddenly engulfs the room as the manic nut case and her reluctant companion are stopped and searched. I turn around to the other passengers and we all crack up, I almost piss myself; it's like watching Beadle About, apart from it is actually amusing. The anger level is now staggering.

Oh well, I'm getting on this plane.

On to the plane and although we are running late, it is no problem for me as the game doesn't kick off until eight in the evening. In fact it only means I could have had a further four hours in bed.

My seat is right at the back and I settle back for a nice kip, until…

Unbelievable, this is not my fucking day! Well there's a nice surprise, the stress ball and chum's seats are next to mine. The anger is in full flow as she sits down, she turns, gives me a glare and introduces herself. Before she has even heard my name she is off in a rampage against all the staff and their families who have ever worked for Air France.

The enemy is soon moved on to BA also, because she thinks one of the girls who welcomed us on to the plane was rude to her. Mmm, I'm not fucking surprised, love.

The sympathetic eyes from fellow travellers who have experienced the wrath of this extremely unhappy woman do not help. Closing my eyes does not help. And soon we're all best buddies playing cards and playing with each other's sexual organs. Can you guess which of the above is a lie? All of them.

The first thing I do is demand a paper from the stewardess, who says she'll bring me one after the safety announcements. I tell her that she is ill informed and she will bring me one now!

She brings me the Daily Mail, I asked for a newspaper and she brought me the Nouveaux Riche Essex Woman's Guide to Life (in the suburbs) or NREWGL as its subscribers know it.

Still, at least it's something to deflect the venomous whore who sits beside me, all I can do is read, block my ears and give thanks to God that this is not a flight to Australia.

Oh yes indeed, this is the most cynical chapter yet.

Via Paris we eventually arrive in Nantes. I thank the almighty and make my way to Beaujoire as the delay has halted my sightseeing for the afternoon.

I go to my regular spot behind the Jules Verne tribune for some grub. Merguez it is then. I sup a couple of 1664's and head to the tribune Loire. The weather picks up and then down; it is properly inconsistent in Nantes as I have stressed previously and all of a sudden we are getting snowed upon. It's not light either, it's bloody heavy and I'm bloody freezing. I think of what my friends would do in this situation, surrounded by people, nobody to talk to and freezing their tits off in a mild blizzard.

Most of them would have walked out and found a bar to watch it on television.

Sauvinaud starts on the left, he is replacing the suspended Armand, who was sent off in Marseille and Fae starts in the middle replacing Berson, who is injured. Again we are playing in 3-5-2 formation. Strasbourg look to be playing in the traditional 4-4-2 and keep out the majority of long balls that Nantes try to float into the path of Moldovan and Vahirua, who must have got over his tantrum in Marseille. The problem is that without Pujol upfront the forwards lack height and knocking the ball down for their attacking partner is close to impossible.

Saying that though, Vahirua gets the ball in the 7th minute and crosses for Moldovan to head just wide.

The heavens open and the Arctic comes to Nantes, and what, five minutes ago, was just bloody cold is now a full on blizzard. The snow is coming down so hard it is difficult to see the players properly. Moldovan has two more chances, but Devauax, the Strasbourg centre back, defends one and the second goes wide.

It doesn't look like the walkover the league placings seemed to have guaranteed. But, it has been one of those seasons. Nantes have played throughout the year with fluidity from defence to midfield, but up front they have (so far) lacked the initiative in front of goal.

The club's personal goal, from the start of the season, was to qualify for Europe. At the moment they are in seventh place and will need to end at least sixth to qualify for the Intertoto cup, so at this point in time this goal is well within reach.

Nantes starts to pass the ball around well in the Strasbourg final third and the defenders from the north are chasing.

Sauvinaud moves down the left and gets the ball to Yapi. Yapi switches to Da Rocha and blam! What a goal, Da Rocha smacks it from outside the area straight past Fernandez, who just clipped it with his fingers, but couldn't stop it. 1-0.

All of a sudden and we are in the driving seat. Strasbourg just can't seem to get a foot in and Nantes comprehensively start to control the game. Vahirua is playing well; he has a point to prove after the Marseille incident and is causing total distress to Strasbourg's back four. It is wonderful stuff to witness.

Vahirua not only starts the attacks by cutting inside the full back, but he chases back and manages to stop most counter attacks also.

Again Sauvinaud takes the ball down the left, he cuts inside and from 20 meters has a go, but is very unlucky as he watches the ball get plucked out of the air by Fernandez.

At half time I head for the mobile canteen at the back of the Tribune and order three coffees. Bloody hell, it is bitter; the weather, not the coffee, but this hot stuff should at least stop my teeth from chattering for a little while.

The second half starts and I move back a few rows from where I had been standing so I can get out of the snow. It doesn't work as the wind picks up and slashes the supporters in the chops, wherever they hide.

Strasbourg as expected, come straight at the FCNA defence, and Ehret, the left back, smacks a well placed shot at goal, Landreau saves and the crowd in the stadium cheer their favourite son once again. Strasbourg attack again, but Nantes defend well every time.

All of a sudden it is our game again and Vahirua takes on Fernanez, but the Strasbourg goalkeeper wins the fight and picks up the ball from little Marama's quick feet. Then Moldovan has a shot but is deflected away out of danger.

I begin to feel comfortable and it looks like three points are in the bag. Half the stadium seems to agree with me and starts to make their way out of the ground and undoubtedly onto warmer climes either in their homes in front of the fire or to the taverns, which wait eagerly for their Euros.

In the 93rd minute Strasbourg get a corner and cross the ball in close to Nantes goal, it looks like Yepes is about to head away, but he is very close to Strasbourg's Kobylik. The ball goes under the bar and into our net. 1-1. I can't tell whether it was Yepes who had the final touch or the Strasbourg player. Damn it.

The whistle goes, and I leg it out of the stade. On my way to the tram, running in a frozen frenzy, I hope it wasn't an own goal because Yepes again played majestically. He doesn't deserve one black mark against his name with the season he has had. He has saved our arses so many times and that would just be cruel.

Still, no matter who scored it, we didn't win, and points dropped at home to Strasbourg is not a good result.

The John McByrne is again totally rammed. But somehow I manage to get a seat at the bar. Joe and Dave will be my company for the evening. I order coffee to warm up and Dave cracks up laughing, I can't stop shivering.

Once I have a couple of beers, a girl comes up to me and asks me if I am the Englishman who comes to Nantes to watch football. Her name is Linda, and she introduces her boyfriend Morgan and their friends Celine and Jerome.

They are all interested in my story, which makes a nice change, as back home, my family seem blatantly bored with the whole idea. They invite me to watch the next game with them, which is against Metz. I readily accept and am already looking forward to watching a match with other people again, and this time with the added ingredient of being able to understand what the hell they are on about.

We become very jovial and they introduce me to more of their friends as they arrive, and explain who I am, and unbelievably one of the newcomers already knows. I can't believe it; I'm famous; well, in the John McByrne anyway. It's a start.

After many a drink they invite me to go along with them to another bar; O'Neil's. We arrive and it seems this is one step too far for my newfound French buddies, as they seem a little too drunk to carry on. Morgan, Celine and Linda all make a move and give me their phone numbers for contact before the next match and agree to meet me in the John McByrne at 6.00pm and take the tram together to watch the Metz game.

Jerome and I get a drink at the bar, some bloke buys me a rum and coke, only for some totally rat arsed young lady to walk passed us and smack it onto the floor (it must be said by accident), Jerome all of a sudden vanishes and I'm alone in unknown territory. I go to get another drink and find that I am out of cash.

Oh well, I don't really need another lubricant and make a move also. The gent who bought me a drink gets me another, or rather demands that the bar staff replace what has been vanquished. I thank him, and then he buggers off as well, is it me or is there a well-known mafia hit about to happen and people are dispersing before the blood hits the walls. I finish my drink and wander outside.

I recognise the area as being not too far away from Graslin and wander back to Georgia's; it's still bloody cold, but at least it isn't snowing any longer.

Bollocks. Still another Saturday and another trip abroad. It's getting to the point when all this is becoming normal. I'm spending loads of cash, but I don't care. It's football and the average man can always find money and time for football. I'm not yet thirty and this could be my final ridiculous extravagance, so I should just make the most of it and worry about the debts I'm mounting up later. After all, those debts would look a lot more grotesque if I never finish what I've started. Wouldn't they?

12

New Mates for Metz

I try Linda's number during the week, but it seems I must have written it down incorrectly as I talk to someone, and she talks back to me, but neither of us have any idea what the other is talking about. Except of course for 'Ciao'.

Oh well, we agreed to meet at the John McByrne at 6.00pm before the Metz match; I just hope her memory is up to it.

Then I phone Georgia and ask her to go to Planete F.C.N.A. to get my tickets for the cup final in Paris.

So off she trots, then phones me back and tells me that I needn't worry I can buy them this weekend, as there are plenty left.

I'm not totally convinced. It is not that I don't trust my sister in law, but I have a feeling that she may have her wires crossed.

I go to bed early on the Friday, but I can't sleep. I'm tossing and turning, wondering if Nantes will charge the Metz defence and if the wondrous cascade of Moldovan goals will continue.

Hetty tells me not to be so sad, and to go to sleep.

Our wedding is now a dead cert and is on for late August.

Our engagement party was last weekend and was a top night. There was only one problem with it from a personal standpoint, and also for a few of my relatives and friends. Arsenal were playing in the F.A. cup quarterfinal and possibly more importantly to me at the moment, Nantes were travelling to Rennes for the Breton derby. The Arsenal game was on telly, and the Gooner contingent of my family strangely enough were running late.

As it turned out both matches went in my favour. Arsenal made it through to the semis and Nantes thrashed their deadly rivals 3-0. Moldovan scored twice and Quint also scored. A thrashing on the Rennais home turf, delightful.

On the next Wednesday Nantes play Rennes again, this time at La Beaujoire in the quarterfinals of the Coupe de France and the same result would be majestic to say the least.

If Nantes can make it to the semis, the possibility of two cup finals in one season and the further possibility of silverware are becoming very realistic. Still, I mustn't get too carried away by it all. We're not there yet.

But you just can't bloody help it, can you? I roll over in bed and start babbling on about this dream end to the season I have envisaged, like so many other supporters. Hetty listens without listening, a skill she has fine-tuned with aplomb this season as I talk to her endlessly about all things yellow and green.

By the end of my conversation with the brick wall that has become my lady I realise she is asleep. I am dejected. If she loves me she should understand, I think to myself.

But just how much of someone else's obsession can you relate to? She is enthusiastic about the writing and also the idea, but she still eyes me with suspicion, hoping that this obsession will culminate and then come to some sort of conclusion at the end of the season.

I haven't got the heart to tell her that it won't, and there is a distinct possibility that it will never end.

There is also a lot more for people to think about right now, this much is true. A bomb has gone off on an over ground train in Madrid. A load of people have been murdered in what at this moment in time looks like a terrorist attack.

It is truly horrific and football again falls from its paramount position at the top of the ladder. Although of course, it will not take too much time for the game to start to re-tread, passing on its way back to the top the more important things in life. Although in this case, it may take a little longer to climb.

The alarm goes off at 4.00 am on Saturday and I feel a lot better than I did a fortnight ago before the Strasbourg match.

I wait for the free bus and one comes along pretty quickly.

At Gatwick the flight is delayed again, but not for too long, so window-shopping and toilet going is called for.

Thankfully this week I do not have psychopathic woman and walkover husband to deal with, which is a right royal relief.

The weather in Nantes is great as I make my way out of the airport to the Tan air shuttle bus, which takes me to Commerce.

Something is slightly different in the Venice of the west this week. There seems to be a fete type thingy on that has overtaken the city centre. Just about every shop has a trestle table outside its front doors, which are crammed with sale items.

I head straight for Rue de Halle and hope that Planete F.C.N.A. are doing likewise. Indeed they are and I buy a t-shirt for next to nothing with the Nantes emblem and the words 'forty years in league one – the record' on it.

I go to the counter to get my cup final ticket. I knew it! Georgia got tonight's lowly game muddled up with the cup final; the final tickets go on sale on the 24/3/04.

I pick up keys from Georgia in her shop in the Passage de Pommeraye during the retail chaos. Georgia explains the street sale is called 'La Braderie' and it commences once a year as a warm up for tomorrow's carnival. Wicked, a carnival. Georgia warns me not to expect too much.

Once I have dropped off my baggage at the flat I head back out into the city as the weather is good and the party vibe is contagious.

A bit of window shopping later and I settle down outside the cathedral St. Pierre with today's edition of L'Equipe.

According to L'Equipe tonight's line up against Metz looks pretty strong.

I look at the defence and at no.6 especially. I wonder how long Yepes will stay at the club if we do not qualify for Europe. I'm beginning to believe he is one of the best defenders playing in Europe.

Lyon play Sochaux tonight and with Monaco not playing until tomorrow against Auxerre, a Lyon win could take them within spitting distance with only a point separating them.

Lyon are still my favourites for the league, Monaco are throwing an awful amount of energy into the Champions League (which you would, I suppose) and I don't think they have a big enough squad to deal with both.

At 5.30pm I head for the John McByrne. Dave and Joe are working and being their usual rowdy selves. I am greeted with 'Alright gooner, you wanker', and so on and so forth. I have become accustomed to such flatteries since my journey began last August.

In stroll Morgan and Linda, my new mates for Metz, bang on time at 6.00pm. Fantastic! I have some company for tonight's game. Actually I haven't.

They will go on the tram with me to the stadium, but they have seats in the presidential stand as Morgan's company are sponsoring this evening's game. I will not have the pleasure of their company later either, as they have free food and drinks at the stadium to take advantage of.

Great, well you kids have a good time, you hear!

At the ground we meet Celine, and then I wave goodbye to Linda and Morgan as they make their way to the lap of luxury.

Celine and I walk into the stadium (Loire end) and we see Jerome. We stroll over to say hello. Now Jerome, from what I could make out on my last visit, is a top bloke, but he doesn't seem to be able to converse unless he is pissed. This is like a few of us, but Jerome literally says, 'Hello' and that is the end of that. I look to Celine for some answers, but she merely shrugs and we find some seats.

In the ground tonight there looks to be around 25,000 and everyone shuts up for the one-minute silence in respect to those who died in the Madrid bombing.

After the silence comes cheers, I turn to Celine and ask for her match prediction '2-0 to Nantes', she responds.

The Metz formation looks heavy on defence, it looks like a 4-5-1 line up.

The game starts and Fae runs with the ball, passes to Pujol. Pujol pulls back a cross for Moldovan, but Metz's defence smother, and then clear the ball.

I ask Celine what she is doing after the game. I realise as soon as I say these words that it sounds like a come on.

But she responds with kudos, noticing my embarrassment, 'John McByrne, probably meet the others later too.'

Armand crosses the ball in, Da Rocha heads it down. Moldovan controls with his chest, turns and shoots into the top left hand corner. 1-0. This is early.

A minute later Metz look like they are going to equalise, Maoulida shoots, but Landreau parries the ball. Noro collects, shoots, but Delhommeau defends well with a block.

Nantes get a free kick on the edge of the Metz box. Armand lines it up. He strikes it perfectly along the turf, past the Metz keeper. 2-0.

At half time I pop back over to see Jerome, he sits uncomfortably, not saying a word. I cannot believe this is the same bloke.

The teams come out for the second half. If we can keep this up, this should be a walkover.

Metz get a free kick. It is miles out though, must be twenty metres from the goal line. Menin strikes it. I do not believe it, top right hand corner. 2-1. A goal and a half. Bollocks.

Of course with confidence high Metz come at us like no one's business, sniffing around for a point. We are chasing the game now.

Ziani starts to get booed by the Nantes fans. He is having a bad game, but this fickle bunch are relentless. I feel sorry for him, as it wasn't too long ago that he was considered too good to be dropped. And that was after Amisse had decided he was free to leave at the beginning of the season. But this blew up in the coach's face when he started to play everyone off the park and became indispensable. So for the fans to give him grief for having a bad run is a little rough. He must feel like he has been kicked in the balls, what with Yapi waiting in the wings to replace him.

Metz counter attack through Gueye, he passes to Maoulida, who beats the last defender and scores 2-2.

NOOOOOOOOOOOOOOOO!

We have thrown it away. Fifteen minutes to go and as much as we try we just cannot score.

Full time.

Celine and I look for Jerome, but he has gone.

We get to the John McByrne and Jerome arrives quickly after us. Pretty soon he will start to talk, but I haven't the time tonight. I have decided it is time to go, I'm fairly shattered and even a couch seems quite attractive.

Back at Georgia's and the place is swarming with artists. Around the table sit the usual suspects, Pierre, Fred, Michelle and a couple of others I don't recognise. They are all from the Beaux Arts (the Nantes art school) in one-way or another.

One of the guys I don't know starts to take photos of me, I'm a little confused, but hey man this is the crazy art scene, I have a couple of glasses of red and crash out on the sofa.

In the morning Georgia tells me I fell asleep with my hands down the front of my trousers and they took photos of me, that bloke is going to use it in an exam piece. Well that's wonderful, can't wait, no really!

Today is carnival day and we have a decent breakfast before the festivities begin. We get maple syrup, crepes and bacon. Georgia thinks it will be totally rank, tries it and thinks it is lovely. It seems North American culinary delights do have something to offer the highbrow gastronomic palette of the French after all; Royale with Cheese anyone?

We sashay through the papers. Looking at the sports section I see we are up to sixth after last night's draw. Lyon closed the gap on Monaco at the top.

Georgia suddenly looks distraught and then tells me what she has just read.

Nantes is in mourning today. The well known and much loved theatre director Michel Liard was killed last night in a car accident. He was driving with his father and his daughter. His father died along with him but his eleven-year-old daughter lived.

David was performing in Ancenis last night when he heard the news, many of his theatre company, including himself, had worked with Mr. Liard. In true 'the show must go on' style they stormed through their set instead of cancelling and dedicated the evening to him. The company were devastated, but put on one of their best performances. This is sombre news, the artistic coterie of Nantes is very closely knit and the pain is obvious.

We walk through the carnival and bump into another artist, Laurent, and his girlfriend; they too are pretty grief stricken by the news.
We decide to have a drink. Laurent, out of all the artists I have met in Nantes, is my favourite. His work is both off the wall and humane. I once saw an exhibition of his, which basically involved photographs, each with a different telephone box on them. At the bottom of each photograph was the phone number of the box. The idea being that you could phone the number from anywhere in the world and if someone picked up you could talk to them with the card in front of you and know exactly where they would be standing. Simple and brilliant.
I talk to Laurent about the writing I am doing about the club and he is very interested. He knows a journalist at Ouest France newspaper who would be interested in interviewing me about it.
And so it is that next time I come to Nantes I will be shadowed by a journalist for the day and the article will be printed in one of the most read newspapers in France. I cannot thank him enough, while trying to remember to keep the mood low.
The journey back to London is short and I manage to make every connection for the first time. My mind is on Mr. Liard and his father. What positives can you take from such tragedy?
The fact that his daughter is alive is of course one, but the psychological damage that comes with it is too much to think about. All you can do is hope that she was not conscious when her father and grandfather were killed.
Almost three generations of one family wiped out in one evening.
Again football is put to the bottom of the ladder.

13

Entente Cordiale

On the Friday night before the Bastia game Georgia phones me to tell me the journalist from the newspaper Ouest France will meet me tomorrow before the match. Her name is Veronique Descalano, David and Laurent will be there to translate.
I jump in the air ecstatically; finally a breakthrough to plug the book or whatever it is to become.
Laurent has come through for me, and I owe him big time.
I find it difficult to sleep, which has become a recurring problem this season. The thought of the interview and answering imagined questions keeps my brain on wake duty.
At Gatwick the plane is once again, delayed, but not by too much, so it gives me some time to munch down some grub.
It is four years today since Hetty and I met, and we should be celebrating our anniversary together. I feel proper guilty, but sacrifices for one's art must be made, and what greater art is there than beautiful football?
At Nantes airport, I've just missed the shuttle bus to the city, so I have 45 minutes to slurp coffee and check L'Equipe for tonight's proposed line up.
There is another anniversary this weekend; it is 100 years since the signing of the Entente Cordiale between France and Britain.
100 years of behaving ourselves and only taking the piss out of one another instead of killing each other.
So this weekend my compatriot, Elizabeth, joins me, better known as the Queen of England. Well I hope she behaves herself and represents the country accordingly, I can't imagine that she packed her bovver boots for the journey anyway.

At Georgia's place the television is on and Chirac and the Queen are strolling through Paris together. Old Jacques, looking more mafia than ever and the Queen looking more like my Grandmother than ever. Georgia seems a bit busy, so I make myself scarce and have a wander around the city.

I go back to the previously visited cathedral St. Pierre; as I walk towards it I can hear singing.

It turns out to be the choir, and is well worth having a look/listen if you are close by. I take a pew inside and listen to these Catholic cheerleaders bigging up the man upstairs.

It looks as though you have to be in the over-seventies club to join the choir, so if you fancy a singsong and are not yet collecting your pension, do not expect any sexual tension in the back row.

When I leave the cathedral the sun is out and Nantes' cathedral square looks fantastic. The main attraction about Nantes, for me, is how it offers both the humble, narrow streets of Bouffay and also have these grandiose wide-open spaces dotted around the city.

Strolling through Bouffay, I pass the John McByrne pub (without going in) and Joe jumps out.

'Oi, Gooner' he shouts.

Joe always seems happy, which is of course a good thing, but not something I am entirely used to with my friends.

He buys me a coffee and we take a seat outside in the sunshine, chatting about football and what has been happening in Nantes. The same old same old as it turns out. If you visit this wonderful place, you must take into consideration that one of its attributes is that it's not the fastest of cities.

Joe doesn't understand why I haven't moved out here yet. My answer is, as you would expect; lack of the lingo and lack of money. I've got a funny feeling that the cleaning/theatre company I work for will not be opening a franchise in the Pays de Loire area anytime soon.

Joe's ambition in life is to open a bar situated between Rio and Sau Paulo and live like a king. He is one of the most well travelled chaps I've ever encountered and he loves these cities equally, if he gets a place between them he has the best of both worlds.

He goes to start work, and I agree to meet him later on.

I walk to the south side of the city, over the river and railway track to La Lieu Unique.

This is an old building, which used to be home to Lu biscuits, but is now a rather trendy arts centre situated on the river.

Inside the building, the design is very postmodern. It has a large gallery space, a café, a restaurant and a shop.

In the shop the magazine '303', (the local arts magazine named after the citiy's dialling code) stares at me. This month it features foreign artists stationed in Nantes. I open it up and there is a massive article on Georgia, I crack up laughing, breaking the trendy silence as I do so. 'Pardon'.

I sit at the bar to toast Georgia's success in this lefty paradise.

A quick shower and makeover for my first meeting with the press since the Eastern Daily Press interviewed me aged 12, while I played one of the Princes in the tower in Richard the Third. It may have been a while, but I'm sure handling hardcore media attention is just like riding a bike, you never forget.

David is outside the café Le Flesselle, which Joe earlier described as "full of arty wankers", in one of his less than liberal minded moments. This is where we are to meet Veronique.

I must seem a little nervous as David reassures me that everything will go swimmingly, and then in the same breath he mentions that Ouest France has a readership of 600,000. Well that's how to settle nerves, that is! I want to tell David that he would never make it as a motivational therapist, but the time passes and it wasn't that funny anyhow.

Laurent and Veronique arrive and the pleasantries, kisses and all things French are done and dusted.

I am asked question after question about football. Who I support at home? Which football magazines do I read? Which newspaper do I get for the best sport section? And so on.

I could get used to this, I have no problem with talking about football for hour after hour. In fact, all I really do talk about is football and music. God, I should do more with my life.

Still, I'm the boss almighty of this situation and the ol' ego is being massaged to absurd proportions.

An hour passes quickly while talking about the city and its team and we realise that we are running late for the match.

We get on the tram, more questions are asked, but I'm only half listening. My mind is on the game now, and I know we will probably miss the beginning. I can't say anything as I am being treated really well, but I'm understandably a little miffed. I don't travel over to this place every fortnight only to miss some of the game, it's priceless time. Still, it's partly my fault for the ego massage and not keeping one eye on the time.

We get to the ground and Veronique picks up the tickets for David, Laurent and herself. The problem is that Veronique's tickets are for the presidential stand, and my season ticket is for the Loire end.

I do not want to miss anymore so, noticing this Veronique does what journalists do best, blag it. They get into the Tribune Loire using the wrong tickets with no hassle at all.

This is David and Laurent's first time at the stadium and also their first football match, David is taken aback by the size of the place. I smile remembering my first time, at Orient.

Veronique and co follow me to where I usually stand, and although I am honoured by the attention, I feel like I cannot relax and that I am being spied on.

I am surprised by the amount of Nantes' first team starters that are in tonight's line up. After all, the cup final is next week and the risk of injury is high in any game.

In the first half Nantes are playing reasonably well, but they can't get past the opposition's full-backs to get in a decent cross.

At half time we all spark up a cigarette, then Veronique decides that now would be the perfect moment for the photograph for the piece. 'Okay, no problem'.

But all of a sudden it is a problem. I, for once, become totally self-conscious. People are staring at me and are looking a little taken aback by the attention I am getting. It feels like the whole of Tribune Loire are gorping at me.

I'm asked to stand in the middle of a group of supporters to give the image an authentic look. I do not know these people and they look a little miffed to be honest.

They are told why I am having my photograph taken by Laurent, they offer me congratulations and everything is all right again.

The second half kicks off, but they want more photos. The problem now is that it is getting on people's nerves. This large flash in the eyes of fans trying to watch the game is not making me the most popular amongst my fellow fans.

But one bloke next to me seems quite happy about the whole thing and we start chatting. After a while he tells me the stadium gossip about who will leave at the end of the season.

It turns out that he thinks Berson, Toulalan, Landreau and Yepes are all off at the end of the campaign.

Blimey, it's a summer sale of the highest magnitude. It could only be gossip though, but if Yepes does stay a lot of people will be very surprised. This geezer next to me actually wants Yepes to leave, for Yepes' sake. That's quite something. A fan that wants the player to move on because he deserved to be known throughout the world and not just in France.

The Corsicans are pushing us back into our own half now, and our breaks are few and far between.

Vahirua has a chance, but misses. He puts it wide after a neat set up from Armand.

It is good to see Vahirua having a go; I hope he is on the way back. Berson picks up the ball about twenty yards out, shoots, but this also goes wide.

On the hour, the subs start to warm up.

Amisse brings on Pujol and Quint for Vahirua and Berson.

The change does make a difference on the attacking side, but without Berson in the middle of the park, Nantes look vulnerable and now have a weak spot.

Bastia, take full advantage.

Gouvernnec has the ball, the Nantes defence stand around and stare at him, they are caught ball watching as he shoots past the diving Landreau. 0-1.

Veronique looks at me sympathetically. I raise my arms in disbelief.

Well, this should give the yellows the kick up the arse they need.

All of a sudden we are on all out attack. Yepes and Gillet are in the Corsican half now.

A cross, Gillet heads, but is well saved.

Yepes crosses, Gillet heads again, but this time it beats the keeper. 1-1. Thousands of us jump up and down on the spot. My new, nameless friend and I embrace.

We get another corner, Gillet heads again, but this time he hits the post.

The last chance of the game falls to Moldovan, but sadly he strikes the ball straight at the keeper.

We saved a point and it was an exciting second half. This is not the best result to take with us into the cup final, but it is of course better than losing.

The four of us leave the stadium and go for a beer at one of the stalls and wait for the tram crush to calm down.

Veronique asks me if I feel despondent about coming all the way here just to see them draw. I explain that I found it harder at the beginning, but I soon got used to the idea that they cannot win all their games.

The final third of the interview is due to take place in the John McByrne (where else?). Inside the pub the smiling faces of Dave and Joe, who look like they are on mushrooms, welcome us.

Laurent asks me to order the strongest beer they have. David and Veronique ask for the same.

Dave the barman looks at them shakes his head and fills up three halves of McEwans export.

They tell Dave that they were expecting pints.

'But I thought you were French' answers Dave.

Blatant racism if you ask me.

So there they are supping on pints of strong ale. This should make my interview a little/lot more relaxed.

After three more pints each, my French friends and I are well oiled.

We talk about football as art (we are drunk). I talk about the great teams such as Argentina 1986, Italy 1982, Arsenal 1989 and they talk about acting and art.

I demand that Veronique mentions the John McByrne pub in the interview, she says she will, and a knowing nod and a free pint comes from barman Dave.

I eventually get back to the flat at 4.00 am and hit the sack.

Sunday morning is a beautiful sunny day, so I head back to the previously visited botanical gardens.

The difference from the last visit is gargantuan as the plants are in bud; ready for another long, hot summer.

They also have deer in the grounds, deer-lerious!

I have a short snooze on one of the benches before heading off to the airport.

The plane lands bumpily at Gatwick and wakes me from my slumber.

On the shuttle bus to the terminal, I check my mobile for messages. I have one from Liv and Laurie. They have had their baby. She is called Vera-Lilly and was born at 9.45 on Saturday night.

Everything seems A-Ok in the health department and all those bellyaches on our road trip holiday have produced a beautiful girl. At least Liv's moaning was not in vain.

I'm concerned that they haven't got any food at home as they would not have been able to leave their flat after the home birth because of tiredness.

Laurie tells me not to worry as he is heading out tomorrow to play football!

'What?'

'I'm going to score a goal and dedicate it to Vera-Lilly. It's what Raul would do.'

Indeed it is, little man.

14

April 17th 2004
The Final

Well hey you crazy kids, it's the moment that we've, or I've, been
waiting for. Could my experiment end in glory and silverware?
Stranger things have happened, and that's a fact.
So it's Nantes versus Sochaux. A big club versus a minnow, a David
versus Goliath kind of trip. The only problem for us is that Sochaux
may well be a smaller club than the glorious canaries, but they are
certainly not a bad one and have not reached the final of the Coupe de
la Ligue by luck. On the contrary, they are one of the outstanding
performers of the year in the league and find themselves in the dizzy
position of fourth place, compared to our seventh, where we seem to
have been plonked for an eternity.
During the week before the big day, I search the Internet frantically to
see if there is any team news, any training schedules, or just anything
at all to do with the final. I need my fix.

Wednesday

At work I'm out quoting for the company looking at various rich
people's plush pads, people who want their cooker to look brand new
on the inside. I want to inform them that they should buy a new oven
and stop wasting my time, but I gladly accept the work and quote it at
twice the amount the job should cost; everyone is happy. While talk of
de-greaser fills the rooms, my mind is most definitely on other things.
I'm far too busy to take work seriously and the team line up for the
cup final looms large in my addled brain. Plus the disasters that could
occur. Never mind the match, I'm still thinking that if one of the key
players puts too much effort into making love to his missus and has a
groin strain, or if Landreau pours himself a cup of steaming coffee

while in mid conversation with a friend and suffers second degree burns on those most precious hands of his. Oh God! What to do?

The key players that I deem indispensable to the team are Yepes, Landreau, Da Rocha and Moldovan. To start without any of these fellas would be suicide.

While rumbling around the nether regions of London on the tube, travelling from quote to quote I scribble down possible line ups:-
Landreau in goal, Gillet, Yepes, Delhommeau as a back three, Armand, Berson, Yapi, Da Rocha in midfield with Moldovan and Pujol up front.

For me this would be the obvious line up. It gives us the best defence we have, although the injured Cetto is supposedly good enough to walk into the team when fit; but sadly that seems to be almost never. Da Rocha has had a great season thus far and is dangerous with the ball at his feet, he also has a strong shot, plus he can feed the forwards. Most of the goals scored this season have been assisted by the no.8 and also by Ziani.

Berson is a strong holding midfielder, although like Gillet he can lose his rag and this could be a problem if the ref is from the card-happy Academy of Annoyance.

Yappi has been a revelation in recent times and all his energy and creativity has given FCNA a different edge to their game since his arrival in January.

Armand is one of the club's major assets and is believed to be off to P.S.G. next year. This is a pity for two reasons, the first being I don't like P.S.G. the second being I see it as a bit of a step down joining the Parisians. More cash and less passion, maybe that is what the modern footballer is looking for.

Armand is a consistent left back/wing back whose major attribute is his cross, and a pretty good shot as his goal scoring record has proven in the past few seasons.

Up front, Moldovan's recent goal scoring spree speaks volumes and, if fit, is a certainty.

I expect Pujol to start alongside him ahead of Vahirua. Pujol is tall and an obvious target man. Moldovan and Vahirua probably just edge it as a partnership when it comes to understanding, but, as they are both small, crossing the ball in from the by line is pretty much a wasted opportunity.

Vahirua had a good start to the season, but the goals and the confidence dried up. It is a real shame as I'm worried he may get the boot next season and he comes across as a good guy.

Xavier told me he once spotted him at the airport, and Vahirua was quite embarrassed by the attention. Xavier asked him for autographs for his kids and he signed all of them with time and precision, asking the spelling of all their names; remember there are five of the little suckers.

Recently Vahirua has been booed by the home crowd, which doesn't bode well, and there was also that paddy at Marseille. On top of all this he hasn't scored for bloody ages and to be honest, I don't see the confidence resurfacing before the end of the season.

Other options for the line up in midfield would be to take out Berson and play Fae instead, just behind Yapi in a holding role. Fae is quick, tough and can also attack. He has a hard, if not entirely accurate shot. If they want to pad out the midfield, Fae and Berson could both start, taking out Yapi. This could slow down Sochaux's rapid counter attack. All in all the result should be tight. Yepes and Gillet will have to play their socks off, but this hasn't been a problem so far this season.

I'm nervous, this much is for certain. Last night I had a nightmare that we lost, but it wasn't against Sochaux, it was against P.S.G. in the final instead. Nantes got thrashed, Moldovan couldn't hit a barn door and the most disturbing factor of all was that Henry was playing up front for the Parisians. Henry was relishing scoring goal after goal against us; it was a personal vendetta against me (it's my dream alright).

Freud would have had a field day...

'So Mr. Rance, you dream that your team is losing to one of your least favourite teams, they are being led in attack by the formidable Thierry Henry, who just happens to be one of the finest living players on the planet, and also the best player in the history of your 'true' team Arsenal football club.

Well Mr. Rance it would only be more disturbing if Henry was wearing a Tottenham shirt and had changed his name to Justin Edinburgh by Deed poll.

Quite simply Mr. Rance, you are scared of losing, and also of winning. To put it bluntly you are scared!

Henry beating Nantes also means, if I may be so bold, that you are a traitor sir, pure scum because you have turned your back on your beloved Arsenal for pastures new, and in France of all places you total and utter wanker'.

Maybe Freud wouldn't have called me a wanker, but I know what he'd be thinking.

Thursday

I'm travelling around the big smoke again looking at print outs from the Nantes website.

The pictures show the team travelling on the bus to Clairefontaine, (spelt correctly?) the training ground of the French international team. One of the pictures showed Yepes and Moldovan leafing through Press Ocean (one of the region's newspapers) and laughing together, looking relaxed. This helped me relax and I caught up with some sleep that evening.

I booked the tickets for the trip to Paris, Eurostar. Two tickets. One for me and one for Xavier. Hetty is slightly miffed, only because she will miss out on Paris, but I emphasise that Xav and I will not see a thing of the City of Light, well, apart from its mother of all stadiums.

Besides, I owe Xav big-time for the amount he has helped me out through the season, plus on the selfish side, who wants to go to a cup final alone? I would have taken Dave and Georgia as well but it would have been a waste as neither of them are into football. I will have to find another way to say thanks to them.

The only deal left on 'lastminute.com' is a hotel plus travel. Xav and I had decided not to sleep and just to take the first Eurostar back in the morning, but booking last minute has not been most advantageous to me this season and it isn't today either.

Oh well, at least if, God forbid, we do lose the last thing we will want to do is stay hanging around in the cold at dawn ready to come home unwashed and unscrubbed. That's okay for Glastonbury, but not for this one.

Friday

As soon as I finish work (yeehah!) I'm off down the Wickham Arms pub in Brockley to meet Laurie and watch Arsenal versus Leeds. Laurie seems well pleased to be able to go out and have a beer after baby Vera-Lilly popping onto the planet. He tells me he has been looking forward to this all week, 'no pressure though. Just make sure it's the greatest night of my life', he says.

Me, a pub, Arsenal on the telly; it goes without saying. And we have come to the right place. The Wickham Arms is probably the only decent pub in Brockley, its competition is mega thin to say the least, but it's one of the last real pubs around. It has loads of different beers, including real ales; that to the non Londoner, might not seem that amazing, but I'm telling you it's becoming extremely common to find the only bitter on tap is John Stiff's Extra Smooth in a boozer. Ooh yummy, I'd rather drink a hot can of Webster's than that shit in a glass.

And it certainly isn't what you call a gastro pub. Instead it only serves bar snacks, but never when you are hungry. However, it always shows the games; just make sure the night you want to see a game is not the night Karaoke is booked, because they turn the bloody sound down to listen to some pissed Millwall fan singing 'My Way'. The Wickham Arms also boasts a superior pub quiz, a dart board, a pool table and a top landlord, who when well soaked is known to buy a round for the pub – result!

I know I'm going on, but it really is a little pocket of paradise, you never get any bother. It's located just at the end of the Brockley conservation area and the clientele is as varied as you will find in any pub; students, labourers, teachers and even a bloke who works at the house of commons mingle, chat and get freely pissed.

Three more points tonight and Arsenal have one hand on the championship; another defeat for Leeds and they are well on the way to being relegated, so if it's an Arsenal win it will give Laurie and I double the pleasure.

By the end of the game, the Gooners have won five – nil. Henry scores five goals, one of which is the cheekiest penalty I have seen in a long time. He runs up to the ball and calmly chips the ball into the middle of the net as the keeper dives sideways. Marvellous stuff.

We decided such a result demanded a celebration and more beer was called for, as we turned it into a belated wet-the-baby's-head night. Laurie told me all the ins and outs of the home birth, which I will spare you.

Saturday

I wake up, pack, and set off for the final.

This will probably be my last time in Paris for a while as there is not much of the season left. Unless of course we beat P.S.G. in the semi-final of the Coupe de France in a fortnight; then I'm right there baby, once more to Paris and the Stade de France.

But one final at a time.

I walk through the streets in the sunny morning down to not so sunny Lewisham to catch the train to Waterloo.

The train is about to pull into Waterloo when my brain pings, jaw drops and the word 'fuck' comes out of my voice box. I've got my passport, the train tickets, but I've left the final tickets beside my computer. I quickly phone home on my mobile, my Godson, Toby; who is staying with us, answers. I tell him my dilemma and tell him to meet me at Lewisham in half an hour because I have to come back for them. 'Well not really' he says, 'I'm about to eat my breakfast'. I won't write what was said, but it was along the lines of 'stick your breakfast in your brain hole'. He hangs up; I hope he's got the message.

I get off the train, and luckily Xavier is on the same train and sees me and also jumps off. 'I thought it was you' he says, 'I heard someone say fuck'. I inform Xav of our problem and we go to the other side of the platform to get a train back. A train stops and we get on, laughing to ourselves about how stupid I have been. The train goes straight past Lewisham. Shit, we've got on the wrong train. The train eventually stops at Hither Green. We leg it out of the station, knocking people out of the way and find a minicab office. We describe our time management problem and the geezer drives as fast as he can. Luckily Toby is waiting for us. I thank him profusely; he calls me a stupid cunt. I love family; the respect is wonderful.

The Eurostar leaves at 11.39. It is now 11.15, and we are in Lewisham. We make it with no time to spare.

Once we have our seats we sit back and sweat heavily. We look at the Eurostar hosts and hostesses and come to the conclusion that they are rejects from B.A. and Air France. They are the cabin crews who suffer from personality disorders and are regulars at anger management meetings. Too dangerous and too useless for a crisis in the skies, but they can be dumped in the tunnel with all the other dregs of European society.

It should be noted that when I normally come to a conclusion like the above, I am wrong.

Xav translates a couple of pages from a French Football magazine and some print outs from fcna.fr (I figure he can't argue, being that I have paid for his trip and match ticket). Once this is completed we head to the bar (of course). The 1664's go down rather well along with a minimal breakfast. After this we have some Duval beers, which are a touch strong, but very good. Weighing in at 8.5% you can't have too many of them if you have a long day/night in front of you. Oops.

The bar is then besieged upon by a bunch of Oxbridge type fellows, who, it turns out, are on a stag trip for one of their comrades. Most seem to be drunk on 'Bolly' and carry a copy of the Times as if it's identification. 'I am a reader of the Times good sir, therefore I like the fact that the working class, when viewing me holding the publication, see me as a thinking man. Because the truth is chum, I only think about me and getting the darned creases out of my Thomas Pink, tallyho!'

One squealing little shit in particular, who can barely get through the door due to his unfathomably large teeth which he sort of talks/chortles through, like a cross between a beaver and Toad of toad hall also carries a copy of The Sun. What comes out of his gob is so unreal I have to order two more beers. 'Look here lads, I've got a Times/Sun combo. Tee hee.' What a Toad of toad hall cunt.

They pass around a blow up doll and pour Bollinger into the plastic ladies vaginal area, then squeeze her torso so the bubbly squirts out like piss, which I must admit I find quite amusing, but I'm fucked if I'm going to let them know it. Then they leave from whence they came, tally ho!

The Eurostar arrives at Paris gare de Nord, and our hotel, The Grand Hotel de Paris, is located only around the corner on Rue de Strasbourg. After taking a couple of wrong turns we arrive.

The room is as small as expected with the budget we are on, but it has everything the travelling football fan requires, a bed, shower and cable T.V. for the football and porn.

It is 4.30pm, the game doesn't kick off until ten to nine, but the stadium gates open at 5.00pm. I want to get to St. Denis, where the Stade de France is, with some time to spare, as I want to sample the pre match delights around the ground as the fans approach and other such gubbins.

We get on the packed double decker train to St. Denis (only one stop). Inside the train is a sea of yellow, but it's not the yellow and green of Nantes, but the yellow and blue of Sochaux. The Sochaux fans have invaded the Paris metro system en masse; Xav and I feel very much isolated.

At St. Denis it is pretty much the same, the ten-minute walk from the station to the stadium is infested with the northerners. There are dozens upon dozens of packed coaches of Sochaux fans, all decorated in the club's colours. A bus drives to our side, the Sochaux fans, see our colours and bang on the windows, demanding a reaction. I take my scarf and kiss it in their general direction, thinking a moony is out of the question this early in the evening. They stick up their middle fingers, what jollification!

I wonder where the bloody Nantes fans are hiding, as this, at first, amusing saunter into enemy territory is not funny any more. The train station must be nearer the south stand (Sochaux's allocated tribune).

One fan pats Xav on the back and says, 'Where have you been, we've been looking all over for you lot?' Piss taking git, but it must be said he has a point; they have turned up in force.

Nearing the north end we see the familiar colours and begin to chill out a bit.

The ground is impressive in size on the outside, but not in design, in fact it's rather bland looking. I'm sure the inside is more impressive, but it is bloody huge, did I say that already, well it is. It's fucking massive, the nearer you get it seems to grow and growl like a huge fat dog. What am I talking about?

I know from the website that 24,000 Nantais are making the trip, but it looks as if the opposition have brought a few more, either that or the neutrals are backing the minnows.

As you would expect many colourful characters soon surround us. Some people have obviously started drinking earlier than us and are a right ol' mess, their face paint already running down their plump cheeks due to sweated out alcohol.

We find a decent looking beer tent (there are at least forty) and grab a couple of pints of pression and a bench to watch the world and its weird and wonderful inhabitants pass us by. I jump to my feet, knock over my pint as I see a load of buses pulling in. The Nantais have arrived. I run into the middle of some Sochaux fans, jump up and down waving my scarf around my head to the Nantes fans, they return the salute by waving flags, fantastic, I'm well up for this.

Xav and I move on, finding a bar very close to the north stand entrance. As soon as we settle in, a green flare is lit and thrown and falls right at our feet, my new silver clima cools turning an attractive aqua-green almost instantly. Xav kicks away the flare and looks down at his own shoes as I crack up laughing; he has one white trainer and one bottle green one. He explains that he got them half price and it makes sense that one should be ruined.

With only half hour until kick off we squeeze our way into the queuing hordes to enter. This is much harder than expected, as the security has closed a few of the entrances and there are loads of us trying to squeeze into one or two gangways. The majority of fans seemed to think, like us, that half hour before kick off would be the perfect time to find our seats. After the crush and jumping around to Nantes songs such as the now legendary 'he who is not jumping is not for Nantes' we manage to get in.

Our seats are in the N17 block, one row from the back of the second tier, so the view is bombastic. The inside is, thankfully, amazing. We seem to have great seats, not that we can get to them, we resign ourselves to sitting on the concrete steps between the seats. So here we are, in a stadium twice the size of La Beaujoire and then some. Wonderful.

Flares are going off in all ends, luckily we have Brigade Loire to our left to keep the momentum going, they have brought plenty of banners and flares, the place is electric, the noise is unreal; both sets of fans seem to want it very badly. A cup final is a cup final after all and as a fan if you can't up the ante for this you are no fan at all. One of the reasons Nantes want the cup so badly is to make history, as they have never before won the Coupe de la Ligue.

The players give the practice balls back to the coaching staff and the ref blows for kick off.

Nantes start well, and although we are not threatening the opposition's goal from the off, we do keep possession. The reason for this amount of early possession I guess is because of the formation. Fae has started instead of Yapi and is playing well in a five man midfield with Berson, Savinuad, Da Rocha on the right and Armand on the left.

In defence the undisputed player of the season, Yepes, plays with Delhommeau on the right and Gillet on the left.

Up front Pujol, the target man, partners Moldovan.

Both sides are looking comfortable amidst the tension.

Around ten minutes in Fae passes to Pujol, who passes to Da Rocha out wide. Da Rocha crosses the ball along the surface to no avail. But Fae picks it up again after tackling the forward, Santos, then passes to Savinaud, who moves to the right side of the pitch, crosses, Pujol is running in to get on the end of the cross: he stretches to reach it and puts it in the net.

'AAghhhhhhghhdllaYYYYYEEEEEEEESSSSSSS, Hhhhsimnerkp[xd[e[d][w[GOAL!!!!!!!!!!!!!!'

Half the stadium screams out in exaltation. 1-0. A guy in front of us in his mid-fifties runs to the front of the stand and pulls down his trousers and pants and slaps his arse in celebration. I jump all over Xav and any other poor git nearby, except Mr. Trouser-less man, I think I'll only go that far if we win.

Oh yes, this is special indeed, this will be a walkover my son.

The delirium eventually dies down as we realise we have almost an entire match to play yet.

The Sochaux captain; Pedretti takes a corner (how the ball even got up our end I don't know, I couldn't see a thing). Nantes can't manage to get the ball and their centre back, Monsoreau, heads straight passed Landreau. 1-1.

Shit, this wasn't in the script.

We were winning the league cup for exactly four and a half minutes. Sochaux then raise their game and are playing well. I'm getting increasingly sick with worry, Xav says it is Nantes' destiny to win and tells me not to panic, I smile, but I'm not one for that destiny, malarkey. As an Englishman, cynicism is my philosophy.

Sochaux have found fifth gear and I want half time to hurry the fuck up. If Gillet and Yepes were not on their usual, almost psychic wavelength we would be behind.

Halftime, come on. Then Amisse can give them a good bollocking and they can come out in the second half all guns blazing. Perhaps Yapi will make an entrance, anything. Please God.

Sochaux get another corner, Christ on a bike! This time Landreau catches the ball on the goal line. Half time arrives.

We dash for the bog. Xav queues up for ages, while I queue for alcohol free Stella Artois, (wife beater without the domestic violence and just the wife). The idea of anything else in our bodies except beer would be too strange so alco-free lager it is.

I get the beers and find a safe spot to plonk them down and spark up a snout. The Nantes fans around me all seem to be generally thrilled, maybe they know something I don't or they are just enjoying a night out, who knows. But I can't smile, I'm shitting it. I haven't felt like this since England were drawing at half time against Argentina in

France '98. Which, of course, we lost; so thinking of this makes me feel even worse.

The great thing though about being a pessimist is it makes those times when you do win all the more enjoyable. Let's just hope this is one such occasion. I calm down a bit as Xavier strolls back; he's bloody smiling too!

He warns me of the massive queue. I wait and sup my pint. Two minutes before the second half is to start I make my way to the urinals. No one there, I have a slash, and come straight back. I am legend, I am Rance. I grab Xav and get caught up in the excitement and mutter something macho and stupid about having a game to win.

We re-plonk our arses on the steps.

Five minutes in and Moldovan watches as his shot is kicked off the line by Flachez.

Again Nantes shoot, this time it is Pujol's turn to be foiled by the goalkeeper, Richet, who is having a good match. Then Sauvinaud has two shots saved in eight minutes.

With extra time looming (92nd minutes) Nantes get a corner, but again nothing works and the ref blows for extra time.

Christ! Well at least we're getting our money's worth. Looking down on the pitch it is hard to see from this distance, but the players look tired and I don't know how many speedy counter attacks the boy Yepes can keep getting back for.

The game starts up again for the first half of extra time. Xav and I walk down to the front of the tier away from some twats that were sitting behind us who kept telling us to sit down. Firstly, they are probably nice and comfy in our seats, and secondly, it's the final for Christ's sake; if you wanted a perfect view you should have sat on your sofa at home with your missus making you a nice brew.

94th minute, Pujol hits a decent shot, but again, no cigar.

Halftime.

We are getting nearer penalties all the time, this may seem an obvious thing to state, but it is a very scary situation. A few of the players are given a rub for cramp and then we are off again.

Moldovan shoots, no bleedin' cigar! Pujol, no cigar, Yapi, no cigar.
This ain't right we should be smoking a lot of bloody cigars, we are all
over them.

All of a sudden there are players all over the shop in the Sochaux box,
Da Rocha, an open goal. Please God, please, please… he puts it over,
his head in his hands. The ref blows. Penalties.

So the result is in the lap of the Gods. I fancy our chances I must say.
Looking at Landreau; ever confident, patting players on the back. This
is the man who got us here really. He saved all those penalties against
Auxerre in the semis, and then had the audacity to score the winner as
well.

Sochaux are set to take the first one. For some reason, I always think
this is the more difficult. The first taker hasn't seen any of his
comrades put the ball past the keeper and doesn't really know where
he is going to place it or blast it until he is at the spot. Saying that, the
penalties are to be taken at Sochaux's end with their fans screaming at
Nantes players, this could be a deciding factor also.

Fran steps up, 1-0 to Sochaux.

Quint, who has only just come on puts the ball on the spot for
F.C.N.A. 1-1.

Isabey is next, he misses (YYYYYYYYEEEEEEESSSSSSSS) 1-1.

Pujol, our goal scorer in the first half, confidence high, could put us
ahead; doesn't. 1-1.

Matthieau the winger takes a steady run and scores. 2-1.

Yepes. If he misses it would be cruelty in motion. He scores 2-2. All
even again.

Pagis scores. 3-2.

Yapis, who since coming on has played well, but even from where we
are standing, he looks nervous. He misses. 3-2.

Lonfat misses too, so we are still in it by the skin of our teeth at 3-2.

Moldovan scores. 3-3.

Diawara for Sochaux, he scores. 4-3.

Armand for Nantes, cool as cucumber, scores. 4-4.

Flanchez kicks the ball and Landreau saves it. 4-4.

Landreau carries the ball out of the goal and puts it on the penalty spot
to take it himself. Without giving himself time to look, he runs up to

the spot and does exactly what Henry did against Leeds last night, minus the skill. He chips it slowly into Richet who simply plucks it out of the air. 4-4.

No Landreau, what were you thinking (saying that, if he'd scored he would be my eternal hero). Landreau now has to get back between the sticks, obviously shattered with despair. Pedretti scores 5-4.

Christ, I want to cry.

Delhommeau must score or we have lost. He misses.

Gutted. Game over.

I can't believe it, I've got to get out of here. I can't watch this other team pick up the silverware. Being sporting is the last thing on my mind as I get out of the ground. Suddenly I remember Xav and have to go back anyway to look for him, now I feel mortified.

The northerners are going absolutely nuts, Nantes fans are crying or screaming obscenities at them. I find Xav and we trudge out without talking, and find the nearest bar. 'Two pints of (de) pression please'. We sulk as Sochaux fans run passed singing 'merci Landreau'. It will be hard to stay angry at Landreau for too long. He is such a huge part of this club and a local hero no less. But for the next couple of nights at least I will unashamedly blame him for tonight's loss. This may be wrong, but emotions are emotions and all I really want to do right now is punch something.

Problem is I'm sharing a bed, in a seedy hotel, with my brother in law to be.

I don't want to punch him; he may get the wrong idea... S&M and all that. He is French after all.

15

Skint

Two games, no money. I've got the fare for the next two offerings, but nowt else, so here is the smallest chapter of the book.
I spent these two weekends before and after the matches sleeping and reading at Georgia's flat.
The first game was against Lille and we won 2-0. Da Rocha scored them both.
Then we played Breton rivals Guingamp and drew 0-0.
What do you want an apology? Forget about it!
The only other thing that happened was that I saw the published interview in Ouest France. The interview was good, but the photograph was diabolical, I looked like a mix between my Dad and Count Dracula.
And my Dad makes Count Dracula look like Robert Redford.

16

The Revenger's Comedy

This coming weekend will be my final trip to Nantes to watch my beloved new club, Football Club Nantes Atlantique, in action.

Well, for this season anyway.

Even that wasn't a dead cert until two days ago when my new credit card came through the door and was activated with £1,500 biggies on it.

The credit card is for my wedding, which if all goes to plan will be on the 28th of August, this summer in Rome.

But, come on, it would be rude not to warm the little financial blighter up beforehand with one last blow out in Nantes.

So the first thing I do with it is buy my flight. Even this moment has a tinge of sadness to it. I go to see the wonderful lady who fakes my student I.D. cards for me then sells me cheaper flights to go with it. A big thank you to you know who you are, you have made things a little less expensive.

In one way the experiment has failed. It, of course, has not turned out cheaper than getting a season ticket for an English club, but to be completely honest it's not far off. On flights and the season ticket for Nantes I have spent in the region of £1750.00.

Okay, so it would have been cheaper at Arsenal, but I couldn't get one and I couldn't face another Orient season, not yet anyway. The plus side to the experiment is quite simple; I have discovered a new club and a new country.

With my final flight ticket in hand I head to work and the first thing I do is check my emails. The journalist who interviewed me for Ouest France, Veronique has come through big time. She has sent me the mobile phone number of Luc Delatour, one of the directors and head honchos at F.C.N.A!

REEEEEEEEEEESSSSSSSSSSSSSSSUUUUUUUUUUULLLLLLLLLLLTTTTTTTT!

Oh my God, this is it! The breakthrough on the last match of the season, it's so Homer man!

I want to kiss that woman, this is beautiful news and I'm moist. Pure genius.

I feel nervous, but at lunchtime I phone Mr. Delatour.

'Hello Mr. Delatour'

'Bonjour' he replies.

'You speeek Inglish?'

No answer, then he realises. 'Mr. Simon Rance, the London fan'.

We have a quick natter, he tells me what I am doing is beautiful and I feel honoured and all that stuff, then he tells me I must call him later as he is in a meeting. He apologises profusely, which is very humble of him, but I tell him it is nay bother and will call back later.

It turns out he wants to give me a special time (Mmm) for the last game of the season, which just so happens to be against Sochaux, that bloody team that beat us in the final. I will get to go on the pitch, have my photo taken with the chairman and the president and be interviewed for the website.

Alrighty!

Marseille represent France in the Uefa cup final against Valencia the same evening. I root for the French, but they lose, after a diabolical tackle by Barthez. He is sent off and the penalty is taken and scored, then it is a Valencian walk over. Oh well.

The night before the game, I chat with Hetty about the last match of the season. She is pleased I have stuck with my beer mat idea until the end. Kind words, considering I missed our anniversary, her birthday and also considering the amount of money I have spent on flights and going out in Nantes (averaging about £250.00 per weekend away), plus the fact that this weekend is coming out of the wedding fund. This fact Hetty will never know, unless of course I have the good fortune of being published.

Well, to be honest, I'm quite proud of myself as well; this is the first independent thing I have seen through to the end. I only wish I could have got to more away games, but getting a credit card was not an option until I paid off my overdraft, which I have only just been able to do.

Even my Dad has come around to the idea of the book recently, which is good for the self-esteem.

My final night bus trip on the free bendy bus is more upbeat than usual too. It still co-stars the usual drunks and kebab chewers but because I know for the rest of the year I will have a lie in every Saturday, I just don't care. Plus my best man to be; Matt (aka Matt Le Shat) has put together a c.d. compilation of loads of my favourite tracks, so I have a soundtrack to my finale.

Joe Strummer's voice and Mick Jones' guitar solo on 'Complete Control' jump around my head as bus punters argue, snore and look queasy. This is what it's all about.

The airport is no longer offering Garbunkle's as it is under refurbishment, so I have to look for artery blockage elsewhere. The problem is, the place is bleedin' rammed this morning. I queue for a rather disappointing croissant and coffee.

The weather in Nantes is piping hot. It's about 22 degrees, which is a lot warmer than back home, but cleverly I have brought some shorts. I am legend.

I dump the bag and go to see Dave. He tells me of a nice place to visit if I've got some time to kill. The river Erdre's bank which is teeming with boats and so on this time of year and is worth a look. Fair dos, sounds like a good one. I won't be able to spend too much time river strolling though, as this afternoon Millwall play Manchester United in the F.A. Cup final. There is only one place to watch such a game in Nantes and that is the John McByrne.

The walk down to the riverbank is quite pretty, and this is also a very quiet part of the city centre and blinding for a picnic type vibe. The walk also takes you past the war memorial, which has the inscription of all fallen Nantais from the wars.

The riverbank takes you through a park and alongside various cafes offering the normal fare. It is very chilled out; I must pass five people in an hour, a little strange for a Saturday.

I make my way back to the city proper, but I still have plenty of time before the cup final coverage starts.

So I head past Graslin and up to the Dobree area, then left past the natural history museum, down to the dockside. I follow the dockside up the hill, and find another residential area, and more importantly, the Museum of Jules Verne.

At the start of the season, this was, apart from the football, the one place I really wanted to have a look at. After all this time and asking people where it is (French people I couldn't understand told me the correct directions, English people didn't care) I bump into it by accident.

There are a couple of top things to know about it. Firstly it's top, and, secondly, it is free and I love a freebie. I can tell you that for free.

It is situated on Rue de l'Hermitage, by the way.

The museum was set up in 1978 to celebrate Nantes' favourite son, and if that wasn't enough for the science fiction guru, F.C.N.A. also named one of their stands after him, now that is respect of the highest order.

In years to come I can see it now: The Tribune Loire Simon Rance, oh yes!

Anyhows, it was set up on the 150th anniversary of Verne's birth.

Jules Verne was born in 1828 and grew up as you can imagine, with an active interest in the arts and literature. The merchant ships, which he watched with awe throughout his childhood, would be coming to and fro docking in the Loire harbour where he once, as a child, tried to stow away on one of the vessels. Large!

There are several displays in the museum to pay tribute to his ideas and the heroes of his books like Captain Nemo and Phileas Fogg.

It is a tribute to this innovative city that it bore a man of such immortal talents.

Back to football, the cup final starts in twenty minutes and I want a bar seat for this one. The John McByrne is, unsurprisingly, full of English. 'Gooner, how ya doin'?' Always a pleasure to see Joe. He screams profanities at the screen and any Manchester United fans who walk in. 'Scum, you're all fuckin' scum'.

He has decided to support Millwall, but points out that they are also scum, but it's northern scum versus southern scum, so he sides with the boys from Bermondsey.

It is another beer fuelled day as swear word after swear word is thrown at the screen, and at one another, in jest. The northern scum inevitably beat the southern scum and lift the cup.

Towards the end of the day one of the Brigade Loire comes in just as Dave starts working at 5.00pm. The BL member gives Dave a magazine. It is a self-published photographic history of twenty years of Loire boisterousness. It features photo after photo of the Ultras over the years having a rowdy time of it, home and away. The Ultra groups featured are the Brigade Loire, Loire-Side (who's emblem is the Lonsdale signal) and Urban Service. It is both a little hardcore, and very colourful. Nantes have a fan base to be proud of considering the size of the town. This is definitely one of *the* footballing cities in France. In fact I think it is the fourth after Marseille, Paris and Lyon. The bloke seems nice enough although we can hardly communicate. I offer to buy him a drink for the magazine. He gives me the magazine and asks for a half of cider, with a half of Leffe (strong pale lager) in a pint glass. I feel sick as I see it poured. I take it to him, he says thank you, and takes a sip and looks a little queasy. I laugh and grab the glass (I'm not having that after looking at those photos of tough geezers in action, I'm not having him not drink this ridiculously expensive pint I've just purchased) and gulp a load, it's vile but I prove my macho point. He does the same and runs out into the street and throws up in the drain.

Oh well, think I better go now, in case any more of the Brigade are around.

Early night it is then.

The next morning is the morning before the big match. I want them to stuff Sochaux for what they did to us. Tonight's opponents though, it must be said, have had an amazing season and have played some of the best football in the league.

Going into this game, there is nothing for us but pride. We will probably go into the Intertoto cup next season just like last season, and then try to make it to the Uefa Cup. We shall see. If they can keep hold of the majority of this current squad they are more than capable.

Tonight is also the night that I meet Luc Delatour et al down at the Beaujoire. I admit I am a little nervous about this.

I have barman Dave coming along with me to translate. He told me last night that he will meet me after the game and we will go to the security entrance and he will translate for the evening.

There are a couple of problems. Today is the Bouffay quarters annual inter bar tournoi. Where basically the teams of the bars start the day with pastis and drink like a right bunch of nutters (under what looks to be blistering sun) and try to play football. Dave didn't finish work until 2.30 am last night, so I am worried what kind of shape he will be in.

I get on the tram towards Beaujoire for the last time this season. Even the things that have become slightly monotonous over the season have all become a pleasure again, like they were at the beginning.

Squeezing onto the tram, eating junk food that repeats on you through the match so you have to keep moving along the walkways so nobody realises it's you, e.t.c.

It is a gorgeous night and the stadium looks wonderful as we approach the golden hour. The fans can be heard in full song while I slurp down my final pre match 1664, which for once is actually cold. The smell of French fries wafts around me, mainly coming from the excellent Chez Robert stall which is located near the season ticket holders entrance.

Inside the ground there is a lot more room than I imagined for the last game of the season, which means I can have a seat for the first half. In front of me this proper pissed geezer is chanting away and burping, while taking bites of a merguez in a roll and sucking the dregs out of a camel cigarette. This is the side of France that Chanel do not want you to see.

Tonight is a big game for a lot of clubs. Our Breton friends, Guingamp, need to win to stay up and our even closer neighbours, Le Mans, could also be relegated.

Nantes start with Landreau in goal. Delhommeau, Yepes and Gillet in defence. Savinaud, Fae, Hadjadj and Armand in midfield. Behind the front two is Yapi and up front, the midfielder Da Rocha and Ahmada. Nantes get straight into the thick of it early on and look like they are as angry about what happened in Paris as the fans are, they certainly mean to make up for it anyway.

Yapi comes out wide and slams a cross along the ground and Da Rocha caps an amazing season by sliding in and sticking it in the back of the net. La Beaujoire is ecstatic. Da Rocha salutes the Loire end and is hugged by Savinuad as the crowd salute one of its players of the season.

A bloke with a drum from the kop, makes his way to the left of the tribune so as to be near the family enclosure and starts banging his drum for the kids, who in unison shout back 'Nantais' between the beats.

In the 35th minute Yapi scores. This is poetry in motion; two of the great achievers of the season have scored against the bastards who took the cup out of our grasp.

The first half isn't all joy for Nantes though. Da Rocha gets a nasty elbow and a tasty storm in a teacup quickly embroils one and all near the incident.

At half time I try to have a look for barman Dave in the kop as I know he will be with that geezer from the Brigade Loire last night who vommed.

No luck though, it isn't the easiest thing to look for a dark haired bloke in a football stadium.

The second half sees Sochaux bring a little more bite to their game as opposed to their handbag fighting. Diawara scores in the 64th minute. But four minutes later this is cancelled out by Savinaud. The full time whistle blows. 3-1. The revenge is complete, they go off feeling a little miffed and embarrassed by their natty little bickering fight and we all celebrate. So we finish sixth, just three points behind Sochaux and as it turns out three above Marseille who have beaten Guingamp 2-0. So sadly Guingamp have been relegated along with Le Mans. This is of course worse for them, but it is bad for Nantes too as they both bring big away crowds to Beaujoire and the extra money I'm sure is much appreciated.

Sadly most of the Nantes players leave the pitch. This is to the total disgust of Yepes, who screams at them to come back. Landreau, Yepes and Grondin (the sub goalie) all walk to the Loire end. Yepes throws his shirt into the crowd, he looks genuinely moved by the support he has received this season and the chants of his name fill the ground. It is then that I realise I will probably never seem him grace the pitch at the Beaujoire again. Landreau throws all kinds of gifts into the swarms of his beloved followers and Grondin holds his baby aloft, a trophy would have been nicer, but still it's a nice touch.

Then they leave and so do we.

I wait outside the ground for any sign of Dave, but hordes of fans are passing by and I realise that I will probably be going alone to the bar to meet Mr. Delatour. Just when I turn my back this thing looking like a cross between one of the Commodores and the Tango man approaches me.

'Alright Si, I'm ready, and I'm not that pissed' says Dave.

I love him.

Christ he is sunburnt though, and what has happened to the hair Lionel?

He rolls up his jeans and shows me how sunburnt his legs are. Christ, he looks like a Scotsman after a month in Gran Canaria, and then some.

We approach the security and Dave strolls up and says in French with a Brummy twang 'This here's your fella from London'.

'Simon Rance!' says the security guard. He motions to another guard and we are quickly whisked away, past the fans waiting for autographs and so on. I pass Oliver Quint as he chats to someone at the entrance to the presidential stand. I could get used to this, that geezer even knew my name.

In fact the rest of the evening, and it's a bloody long one, involves people coming up to me, shaking my hand and telling me what a great thing I am doing by coming over here to watch Nantes. It is pure bliss; they push the boat out entirely when I am introduced to the President and the Chairman. Franck, the resident F.C.N.A. journalist introduces himself and asks if he can have an interview. I say of course, and we sit in the presidential bar supping free beers and having a natter.

Dave watches from the bar as I am asked questions, waiting to translate if need be, but there isn't any need as Franck's English is excellent. Dave just laughs, as it seems he is not going to have to do too much tonight apart from sup lager and watch me.

Luc Delatour has sorted all this out, and he is the most entertaining host I have known in a long time.

I seriously thought the night would end with a free beer and a handshake, then a 'go on, fuck off'. But they took me around the changing rooms, onto the pitch, took my photograph for the website, gave me more beer, and more beer, and more beer.

I had a long chat with Luc Delatour, whose enthusiasm for the club is plain to see. He agreed with my vote for top three players of the season, Yepes, Landreau and Da Rocha.

Another plus was the club's looming interest in the book I told them I have written about the season.

They want to read it, and then well, who knows.

I don't know what time Dave and I left, but we were dropped to our respective front doors after a top night at the hands of F.C.N.A.

Dave turned around at his door and said to me 'What the fuck was all of that about?'. I shrugged in self-satisfaction and my driver took me home. Result.

The next morning I tell Georgia about my amazing evening, then we have a final lunch together in Bouffay before I have to head for the airport.

On the plane I try to reflect on the season, but I'm so bowled over about what's just happened that I can't.

It has been a wonderful experience for me, culturally, to spend so much time in another part of Europe. I know the streets of Nantes better than those of Lewisham Borough now, that's for sure.

But I don't really know what I have learnt. Whether I was supposed to learn anything in the first place I don't know (a bit more French may have helped).

All I know is I love football, and like any football fanatic I cannot get enough, and all this trip has done is make me hungrier for more.

This game is so beautiful and the world is so big that to confine one's passion to just one club and one country is a waste.

I'm looking forward to seeing Hetty, I'm looking forward to some weekend lie-ins, I'm looking forward to getting married, but most of all I'm looking forward to next season.

Allez.

Final Standings for French League One 2003-2004

Pos	Club		Points
1	**Lyon (OL)**		**79**
2	**Paris (PSG)**		**76**
3	**Monaco**		**75**
---	---	---	---
4	**Auxerre**		**65**
5	**Sochaux**		**63**
6	***Nantes (FCNA)***		**60**
7	**Marseille (OM)**		**57**
8	**Lens**		**53**
9	**Rennes**		**52**
10	**Lille**		**51**
11	**Nice**		**50**
12	**Bordeaux (Girondins)**		**50**
13	**Strasbourg**		**43**
14	**Metz**		**42**
15	**Ajaccio**		**40**
16	**Toulouse**		**39**
17	**Bastia**		**39**
18	**Guingamp**	**R**	**38**
19	**Le Mans**	**R**	**38**
20	**Montpellier**	**R**	**31**

Lyon win the league and are joined by PSG (Coupe de France winners) and Monaco in the Champions League next season. Auxerre and Sochaux (League Cup winners) will play in the Uefa cup. FCNA will play in the Intertoto Cup.

FCNA goal scorers for season 2003-2004

Moldovan	11
Vahirua	7
Da Rocha	6
Pujol	6
Armand	3
Berson	2
N'Zigou	2
Ziani	2
Gillet	2
Fae	1
Glombard	1
Hadjadj	1
Quint	1
Savinaud	1
Yapi	1

FCNA league results 2003-2004

August
Sochaux 2 FCNA 1
FCNA 2 Lens 0
Ajaccio 1 FCNA 3
FCNA 1 Le Mans 0
FCNA 0 Bordeaux 0

September
Nice 1 FCNA 0
FCNA 1 Marseille 0
Strasbourg 1 FCNA 0

October
FCNA 1 Rennes 0
Metz 1 FCNA 3
FCNA 0 Lyon 1

November
Montpellier 4 FCNA 1
FCNA 0 PSG 1
Bastia 1 FCNA 3
FCNA 0 Monaco 1

December
Lille 2 FCNA 0
FCNA 1 Toulouse 1
Guingamp 1 FCNA 1
FCNA 1 Auxerre 0

January
Lens 0 FCNA 0
FCNA 4 Ajaccio 0
Le Mans 0 FCNA 1

February
Bordeaux 2 FCNA 0
FCNA 3 Nice 1
Marseille 1 FCNA 1
FCNA 1 Strasbourg 1

March
Rennes 0 FCNA 3
FCNA 2 Metz 2
Lyon 1 FCNA 0
FCNA 3 Montpellier 2

April
PSG 3 FCNA 2
FCNA 1 Bastia 1
Monaco 0 FCNA 1

May
FCNA 2 Lille 0
Toulouse 0 FCNA 1
FCNA 0 Guingamp 0
Auxerre 2 FCNA 0
FCNA 3 Sochaux 1

FCNA CUP RESULTS 2003 – 2004

Coupe De France

4/1/04
Beaujolais Mont d'Or 1
FCNA 2

25/1/04
Fontenay-le-Comte 0
FCNA 3

11/2/04
FCNA 4
Brest 0

17/3/04 (QF)
FCNA 3
Rennes 2

28/4/04 (SF)
FCNA 1
PSG 1
(PSG won 4 – 3 on penalties).

Coupe de la Ligue

28/10/03
FCNA 3
AS Nancy 1

17/12/03 (QF)
FCNA 1
Clermont Foot 0

14/1/04 (SF)
Le Mans 1
FCNA 1
(FCNA win 5 – 4 on penalties)

17/4/04 (F)
FCNA 1
Sochaux 1
(Sochaux win 5 – 4 on penalties... Gits.)

Bibliography

The Rough Guide to European Football.
Peterjon Cresswell & Simon Evans.
Rough Guides.

Nantes.
T. Guidet & H. Cayeux.
Editions Ouest France.

Brittany.
Philippe Barbour.
Cadogan Guides.

www.fcna.fr

FIN